Table of Contents

Foreword by Scott McLeod, J.D. Ph.D., Iowa State University 3

Acknowledgements 5

Introduction: Why Habitudes 7

Habitude 1: Imagination 15

Habitude 2: Curiosity 31

Habitude 3: Self-Awareness 49

Habitude 4: Perseverance 63

Habitude 5: Courage 79

Habitude 6: Adaptability 99

Final (Starter?) Thoughts 115

Afterward by David Armano 119

Appendices

Habitude Awareness: The Unchecklist 123

Worksheets & Graphic Organizers 127

Internet Resources 147

About the Author 149

Foreward

By Scott McLeod, J.D. Ph.D., Iowa State University

http://www.dangerouslyirrelevant.com

The world in which our students are growing up is nothing like the world of previous generations. Today's children have never known a time when the Internet and personal computers didn't exist. They have never experienced an environment devoid of cell phones, iPods™, Facebook™, and YouTube™. To those of us who remember when the news was on paper and when books couldn't be downloaded from thin air, this first digital generation is an often baffling (and sometimes frightening) group. Yet it is these students that will transform the ways we work and play, the ways we live and think.

As stewards of the next generation's educational opportunities, we have a responsibility to prepare them for their world. Not our world, but theirs. If the world is now technology-suffused and globally interconnected, then we must adapt our schooling practices to reflect those facts. If global workforce demands require a different generation of employees, then we must provide it. We cannot continue to prepare students for a world that no longer exists.

That's why this book is so important. Labor economists continue to compile the hard data that the well-paying jobs of tomorrow will require different skill sets. Demographers continue to show us that creative, talented workers are more than willing to relocate, transforming previously thriving communities into global backwaters. At some point we have to listen to our experts, retool our educational systems, and reorient our ways of thinking.

Angela Maiers understands this new world. She recognizes that future citizens and workers must be critical problem-solvers and effective collaborators. She knows that this generation must be information-savvy, technology-literate, and globally aware. Most of all, she sees that a rapidly changing world requires that we train our children to be courageous and adaptive. But we don't do that by having them spit back to us "the right answer."

This book is about retraining your own mind. It's about shifting your own way of thinking about schooling to a 21st century model and seeing, in concrete terms, how that might play out in practice. Read through Angela's Habitudes. Reflect upon their significance for today's educational practices. Share with others that the world has changed. And then go out and do something about it.

Scott McLeod, J.D. Ph.D.
Associate Professor, Educational Administration
Director, UCEA Center for the Advanced Study of Technology Leadership in
Education (CASTLE)
Iowa State University

Acknowledgements

This book is a testament to the Habitudes! Taking more than three years to complete, it has been a true labor of love representing my respect for teachers and what they can do, and my passion for students knowing what is possible.

Writing this could not have been possible without the help and support of many. I have had the opportunity to observe, collaborate, and work with truly remarkable teachers and administrators who have taught me so much about teaching and learning. Their work with children has given me inspiration and a deeper understanding for what it takes to this job well. I am honored to call them my colleagues and friends.

Finally, I would like to thank my family, especially my husband Bob. I know the many nights of writing and time away from our family was not easy. As I watch our children Ryan and Abby grow, I am inspired each day by the joys that they encounter and the way their minds work. They are what fuel my passions and conviction to continue this dialogue with students and teachers every day.

Introduction: Why Habitudes?

"The only thing that interferes with my learning is my education." - Albert Einstein

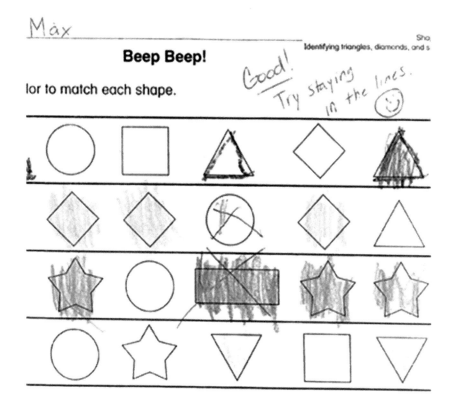

A friend of mine shared with me the following story:

"Daddy, daddy! Look what I did! "

That's awesome Max!" his dad replied, as any parent would. They were looking at one of young Max's assignments; coloring and matching shapes. Typical stuff, he thought as his five-year old skipped away. But upon closer examination, he looked at the paper a little longer, and he couldn't help but notice the teacher's comments.

"Good Job, Max! Try staying in the lines."

Dad's afterthought was this:

"I understand that kids need to learn how to color in the lines. It teaches them basic coordination and concentration. But what does it teach them about themselves? What does it teach them about skills that might serve them well one day in the real world?

Couldn't there be an assignment in addition to coloring shapes that maybe included handing them blank sheets of paper and asking them to invent and name a shape that no one has ever heard of before? Maybe some kid would come up with a Sqoval, or a Tri-square, or even an Octocircle. Who knows? The point is that we do need to be taught to do things like coloring shapes at a young age, but shouldn't we also be taught how to invent, create, and look at problems from a totally different perspective?"

Thanks to David Armano, for sharing this story. It illustrates how accountability, standardization, and conformity all work together keeping our learners within the lines, and on course with our objectives. But, he's right, does this agenda interfere with the kind of learning we desire most?

Checklists have dominated our education system for decades. Our checklists determine what our students "have-to-do, have-to-know, and have-to-be." Obedience, order, and sequence have become the laws of learning. Those excelling -- our "good" students -- diligently fall in line with our checklists, proving they hear what we deliver, remember what we say, and answer what we ask.

As a teacher I understand. In a world with mounting pressures to "get things done," checklists have become our salvation. I love them too! There is an exhilarating feeling that occurs after each mark is successfully checked off. The harder the task, the harder the check mark, right?

Yet, I wonder, is the checklist we operate from, our scope and sequence of traditional skills and lessons, enough for our students to invent, create, collaborate, and solve their own problems?

This book is not about adding more to our lists of HAVE's, DO's , and BE's, but rather thinking outside the line and intentionally about BE's, DO's, and HAVE's that matter most. The 21st century world needs our readers to BE critical, BE creative, and BE strategic. The 21st century world demands readers to DO their own thinking, rather than relying on someone else to think for them. The 21st century world expects leaders to HAVE the endurance, fortitude, and courage to brave through each new challenge with confidence and competence.

So, let's uncheck this list and explore together the behaviors, habits and attitudes – the Habitudes -- that we know with conviction will ensure our students for success both inside and outside our classroom walls.

HABITUDE 1: IMAGINATION

A cardboard box; a basket of unfolded laundry; an individual blade of grass. To a child, these everyday unnoticed items become a fort, clothing for a king and queen, and a harmonica that plays symphonic music. Imagination is not just for kids. Discovery, innovation, creativity, and learning all begin with imagination. Everyone says imagination is important, but it's something we take away by forcing students to memorize and repeat rather than think and envision.

HABITUDE 2: CURIOSITY

Champion learners are curious about everything. They ask questions and get themselves involved in all stages of learning without worrying about the answer, but relishing in the process. They have learned that by posing questions, they can generate interest and aliveness in the most exciting or mundane situation. This inquisitive attitude fuels their unrelenting quest for continuous learning.

HABITUDE 3: PERSEVERANCE

I think of times in my life it took more than "I think I can" to get me to my goal. Most recently, I completed running in my first half marathon. Without resolve, determination, firmness, and endurance, I know I could not and would not have physically or mentally gone the distance.

HABITUDE 4: SELF AWARENESS

We all have strengths and weaknesses in regard to our learning performance and capabilities. Knowing yourself, knowing your strength, preferences, and areas of need is a critical characteristic of a successful learner. Yet, self-awareness is more than just recognition of what you can or cannot be, do and have. This innate ability to stay in tune serves multiple purposes. They can foresee problems and use their strengths to overcome difficulties encountered.

HABITUDE 5: COURAGE

Courageous learners understand that safe is risky. Success is the byproduct of taking risks, closing our eyes, saying I will not let fear hold me back and taking the plunge. I want them to understand that it takes courage to address the voices in your head that echo doubts, questions, or other paralyzing thoughts.

HABITUDE 6: ADAPTABILITY

Adaptability is more than just serving change; it is using change as a growth opportunity. In fact, with anticipation of change, you can control change. This kind of development requires robust adaptability. The world opens up for adaptable learners, as they approach each task and challenge willing to be a beginner.

They approach their learning and life with a beginner's mindset. These learners embrace challenges with openness and flexibility. Those who don't embrace change with adaptability usually get blind-sided by it.

Care to join me as we step out of the lines?

NOTE TO THE READER

In Classroom Habitudes, I'll present the scope, and you will decide the sequence. This is not a checklist-like book, so I am not going to tell you how to read it. What I will do is share with you the format of each chapter, so you can start with any of the six habitudes. In each chapter, you will find the following to help support your conversations with students and colleagues:

Introduction: Each chapter will begin with a brief introduction to each habitude outlining the focus of the chapter and the lessons within the chapter.

The Porch Pitch: In the last decade, people relied on the elevator pitch, selling your idea in the amount of floors it took the elevator to go up. In today's quick attention span generation, we have to be able to deliver a "porch"-quick theory, concise and succinct. This section represents the habitude porch pitch answering the question: Why does this matter to me?

The Million-Dollar Conversation Starter: Each conversation we have with students in some way "deposits" knowledge and experiences that can be "withdrawn" for future use. We regularly have discussions with our readers about how text work and strategies they can use, but are we including in those conversations knowledge and awareness of the habits, attitudes, and behaviors of successful literacy learners? Do we deliberately and explicitly teach ways to explore and uncover the valuable lessons that ultimately shape our character, integrity, and resolve as lifelong learners? These habitude-driven discussions are what I call "Million Dollar Conversations."

This ANCHOR lesson is the first full conversation I have with students launching the study of the habitude. This lesson starter is fully scripted so educators can get a feel for what the conversation might sound like with students. I have taught each anchor lesson in multiple grades and content areas, therefore some pictures, student work, and responses may be included in the description.

Conversations that Last - Continuing the Dialogue: No habitude can be "mastered." It develops over time and with practice. Each chapter will include several habitude lessons that provide specific ideas and tools to develop and nurture the habitude. These lessons do not follow a prescribed scope and sequence. They can and should be expanded and extended over days and weeks. These conversations keep the habitude alive and moving, so students link the habitude in their both their deskwork and life work.

The Take Away: After all the lesson and habitude conversations, these are the key points or messages I want students leaving with. If they can "take away" these ideas about each habitude, the work we have done in class will serve them far beyond the classroom walls.

Reflections: As teachers and administrators we are the models we wish our students to be. To help us reflect on how each habitude enhances our reading and learning, I have provided a series of questions for reflection.

Resources: I have included a list of text and web based resources to support the teaching of each habitude.

Habitude #1:
Imagination

Imagination is
the foundation
of all thinking.

Without seeing
the possibility,
we cannot achieve
the outcome.

HABITUDE # 1: IMAGINATION

"Imagination is more important than knowledge itself."
- Albert Einstein

What is imagination? How does imagination work? Can it be taught? If so, how do we go about doing that? These are the kinds of questions philosophers and theorists have spent centuries pondering and ones I seek to answer for this critically important habitude.

Imagination has been defined and associated with the ability to form images, store memories, create illusions, and visualize new realities. If we take all that together, our definition might go something like this:

Imagination is the mind's ability to constantly create images containing thoughts and memories ignited from our senses. In those images, we create our ideals, role models, heroes, loves, concepts, perceptions, and ideas on how to thrive and survive.

Life then is exactly what we imagine it to be. So, let's explore with students how far their imaginations can take them.

Porch Pitch: Why Imagination Matters

There are only three pure colors: Red; Blue; Yellow. But look at how Michelangelo imagined these colors into majesty. There are seven musical notes, yet hear what Chopin, Vivaldi and Mozart created from them. Imagination is the active ingredient in making all this happen.

Imagination is the foundation of all thinking. If we cannot see the possibility, we cannot achieve the outcome. Imagination is our mind's eye with the capacity to jump from present facts to future possibilities. Our capacity to dream, hope, and plan for the future is influenced and impacted by the control and understanding of imagination's remarkable power.

- Imagination helps us learn about ourselves and the world around us.

- Imagination helps us cope with and solve problems.

- Imagination helps us become more creative.

- Imagination makes it possible to experience a whole world inside the mind, enabling one to mentally explore both past and future.

Million Dollar Conversation Starter (Anchor Lesson):

Good Morning Boys and Girls,

Two words important to learning: Knowledge and Imagination

(Give students time to talk and discuss the relationship between the two)

Knowledge is what we know. Knowledge represents what we have learned and mastered.

Imagination is how we use our knowledge and experiences to envision the future. Imagination allows us to see life as it would or could be. Here is what Albert Einstein said about the two, "Imagination is more important than knowledge itself."

Why do you think he felt that way? Do you agree?

(At this point, I allow the students to engage with each other in conversation, creating a community of imaginative learners. Remember, collaboration plus competition can equal greater creativity.)

Successful learning is more than just absorbing and remembering information. Understanding in school and in our lives requires many different parts of our imaginations. In fact, imagination is so important it has been called "the most essential tool for human intelligence." Here's why: With it we can invent new realities. As we explore the habitude of imagination together over the next days and weeks, we are going to be learning about tools important and related to imagination: imaging, visualizing, creating, and innovating. With these tools there is no limit to what our imaginations can do.

Think about this for a minute:

Everything new...every invention...every idea...every improvement in our life comes from our imagination - not from our knowledge!

It's not so long ago there where no cars...no airplanes...no...Internet...and yes... no video games! All these groundbreaking revolutions started with the power of the human imagination - not human knowledge! Until someone imagined it, none of the things you know and use would be real.

Today, we are going to explore this amazing thing we call our imagination by taking a look at how it works and how using it wisely can help you improve your life in school and out. Are you ready to do that? I want you to relax and close your eyes. Use your imagination and try form a picture in your mind of the following scene. Listen carefully to the way I prompt and prod your imaginations to help you get the image as clear as possible.

You are a part of a team of world famous mountain climbers and you have just reached the peak of Mount Everest. You have attempted this dangerous and challenging climb twice before and failed. After seven long, grueling weeks, you are there! Put yourself in that spot, right at the very peak! Can you see yourself there? Keep your eyes closed. Focus and visualize yourself standing there. I am going to challenge you to really concentrate. What are you wearing? What does the equipment on your back feel like after climbing all that way? Feel your arms and legs-how would you describe them? How about your face? Can you see your breath? Take a deep breath in and describe the smells. Now listen, what do you hear? What are your teammates saying? How do their voices sound? What emotions are you experiencing? How would you describe those feelings? Stay really still, freeze that moment in your mind.

Okay, I need you to open your eyes for me. How do you feel? Anyone exhausted? What sense was strongest for you? What made the image clearest and most real?

Make sure that you ask questions about the senses without directing which sense they should feel most. Everyone has different sense strength, so let the imagination flow and grow.

Now, let's try something a little less strenuous. I call this the lemon test. It goes something like this:

Imagine you're in a kitchen and there's a bowl of fresh lemons. You take one and place it on a chopping board and slice it open. Can you smell that fresh, lemony fragrance as it sweeps up to your nose and spreads across the entire room? Slowly pick up the lemon and open your mouth . . . that's right . . . and squeeze in a huge mouthful of juice.

Can you taste it?

At this point in the lesson, I can clearly see their puckering faces and know for sure their taste buds are working.

Boys and Girls, as you think about these simple exercises, what did we learn about the power of our imaginations today?

Your imagination may be all in your head, but its effects can be felt all throughout your body, don't you agree (say yes!)?

- Here are some things I would like us to consider and reflect on for tomorrow:

- What did you learn about your imagination today?

- How can having a good imagination influence your learning?

- How do you use your imagination now?

Lessons that Last: Continuing the Dialogue

Imagination cannot be "mastered." It develops over time and with practice. The following imagination lessons provide you with specific ideas and tools to build imagination. These lessons do not follow a prescribed scope and sequence. They can and should be, expanded and extended over days and weeks. These conversations keep the habitude alive and moving, so students link imagination in their deskwork and their life work.

Lesson One: Creativity & Imagination

- Galileo made his first important scientific observation at 17.

- Handel composed music when he was 11.

- Concert singer, Marian Anderson began her singing career at age 6, teaching herself how to play the piano at age 8.

Incredible discoveries and achievements have been made by people in their early years and teens. Right now, our students' brains are ripe and ready to create new and brilliant ideas, so this is a great time to talk to them about things that will enhance their imaginative and creative abilities.

Boys and Girls,

Today I want to talk to you about creativity and its link to using your imagination in productive and powerful ways. Creativity involves your ability to take the thoughts and ideas you imagine and turn them into something you want. You already are creative. Do you remember when you were younger and you could take an ordinary cardboard box and turn it into a fort? Or take a bathroom towel, become a superhero, and fly around your house? That is creativity and imagination at work.

Creativity doesn't stay strong without work and commitment. Like any other mental process, it takes practice to get good at it. Believe it or not, one of the best ways to get your imaginative and creative juices going is to play a game. Games are one of the best tools creative people use to come up with their ideas. Creative playing leads to creative thinking and often leads to creative results. Sometimes adults forget to let you know the importance of playfulness, messing around, and trying out new ideas just for the fun of it! Some grown ups have lost their "creative spirit," but I know you all have not...so lets play for a bit, shall we? This game is called "How Come?"

Here's how it works. I'm going to describe a situation or setting. Your task is to answer the question, "How Come?" with as many creative scenarios as your imagination will allow. Push yourself to stretch beyond the obvious.

Here's the situation:

Mrs. Maiers went to a school in the middle of the day, in the middle of the week, but she didn't see any children there. How Come?

_____   _____

_____   _____

_____   _____

_____   _____

_____   _____

_____   _____

_____   _____

_____   _____

_____   _____

Did the students persist until all possible scenarios were explored? Were they able to get past the common answers of a spring break or fire drill? How soon did they come up with the far out answers such as alien invasions? Which group first came up with different kinds of schools -- like night school, or a school of fish?

Certain games and puzzles can furnish your students with plenty of opportunity to flex their creative muscles. Games like chess and checkers are great as they both force students to map out strategies and make moves that depend on what an opponent would do. Interactive games like Cranium™, Pictionary™, and Gestures™ provide great creative exercise in thinking up novel ways to communicate and compete.

Lesson Two: Imagination and Problem Solving

"One should not put pencil to paper before having visualized what one wants from all angles... I have come to work by a series of mental images... the drawing board enables me to give effects to those images."- Ettore Bugatti

Everyone has problems. They can be small things like, what shoes am I going to wear today (this is actually a common problem for me). Or how am I going to get this assignment done by Friday (perhaps a common problem for you)? Luckily, you have what you need to solve almost any problem. You guessed it… your brain and your powers of imagination. Successful problem solving takes more than gathering information. It requires looking at the problem from many different angles, upside down and inside out.

Finding imaginative solutions to the challenges and difficulties is not an easy task. We will practice this together often. The work we do will not only help in school, but will become a strength for you long after our conversations are over. Being a successful problem solver is one of the most important skills you will use outside of school.

Here is what I see happening often, even with grown ups. When confronted with a problem, people often try to 'force' their brain into coming up with a solution right away. I am going to model for you a better system for working through problems using the powers of your imagination. It is called Mind Mapping (adapted from the work of Tony Buzan), which is exactly what the tool does. It maps out the things that I am imagining would be or could be. In a Mind Map, I can contain all the elements of a problem in a single visual 'take." It allows me to see the color, shape, and sound of my problem and its possible solutions. Let me show you how it works on a problem I have been having. (You may share with students the example included in the Appendix or share with them your own personal mind map.)

- Here's how the Mind Map Works:

- I start with the problem, it is my central image.

- I create the branches to represent possible solutions.

- I share my mind map with others, so that as we talk they can add "branches" that stretch and grow my thinking as well.

Imaginative problem solving does not make my problems and challenges disappear, but it does allow me to see problems in a different ways. Each time I work out a problem in this way, my thinking and my brain get stronger. I am able to tackle bigger problems with more efficiency and confidence knowing there is always more than one way of working it out.

Lesson Three: Imaginative Reading

Reading is one of the strongest ways to develop your imagination. Great readers do not just read the words in a book; they envision the world of story in their minds. By creating images, they are able to understand and relate the writers' ideas to their own lives. Imaginative readers are able to literally step inside the story. Imagination transports them into the story's world, where they can envision the setting, the characters, and events.

Imaginative reading involves more than just getting lost in the text. As readers step into the roles of the characters and move around in their world, the text literally comes alive in their mind. To enter the story's world, learners are required to move from a passive stance to a more active role in the reading and thinking process. Drama and enactment strategies are a powerful way to take even the most reluctant reader from spectator to participant.

You can begin to introduce these strategies even in simple stories. A favorite of mine is called Revolving Role (adapted from the work of Jeff Wilhelm).

Here's how it works:

Students pair up and each partner assumes the role of a story character. During a particular scene, students are asked to "enact" or briefly dramatize that scene from their characters' perspective. As students dramatize that scene in pairs, they explore what each character might say, do, feel, believe...

Students can exchange partners or roles several times during the reading. This allows each student to view the story from a different perspective and discuss how they believe the characters would now respond to a certain problem or dilemma.

Throughout the story students are expected and taught how to talk, write, reflect, or represent their understandings of the text, author, characters, and themes.

Let's give it a try with the classical favorite, "The Little Red Hen."

After reading or retelling the story, have students select a partner.

Student A is the Little Red Hen. Student B is Little Red Hen's Mother.

Pause at the point in the story where the Little Red Hen asks all her friends to help her bake the bread, and they all say no. Have students visualize that Little Red Hen then runs home to talk to her mother. The enactment begins at this moment. Have students recreate that conversation with their partner, and then share as a whole class.

Reverse roles. Now, Student B becomes The Little Red Hen and Student A is mom. The next enactment occurs at the end of the story when all the animal friends have smelled the bread, asked for a bite, and Little Red Hen says no to them. While she is eating her hard work, her mother comes by and has something to say. Have students enact that conversation.

Conclude the discussion by having students share their understanding of the story from multiple perspectives. Discuss with students what it felt like for them to take on the "roles" of characters within the events in the story.

As students get more comfortable with enactment, they will become more involved in the imaginative story world making their reading experience deeper and more powerful. Over time, I expect students to rely less on physical enactment and rely more on mental engagement with the text using their imagination to guide them.

Lesson Four: Visualization & Imagination

Imagination is the ability of the mind to build mental images of scenes, objects or events that are not present or have happened in the past. It involves all the five senses and full emotion. One can imagine a sound, taste, smell, a physical sensation or a feeling or emotion. For some people it is easier to see mental pictures, others find it easier to imagine a feeling, and some are more comfortable imagining the sensation of one of the five senses.

"Imagine the Music" is a powerful exercise of the imagination, giving students practice using their imagination in focused and controlled ways. This exercise is intended to heighten student's power of visualization by engaging the senses.

1. Select two different kinds of music or songs from different genres (rock, country, jazz, classical, etc.).

2. Explain to students the purpose of the exercise will be to practice and refine their ability to visualize by using the strength and power of their senses.

3. As the music is played, use the following questions to guide the reflection and discussion:

    If you were to sculpt the song, what materials would you use?

    How does this song smell?

    What shape would it make?

    If you could take a bite of this song, what would it taste like?

    What color is the song?

    If the song were an animal, what would it be?

Giving color, shape, texture, taste, and feeling to the invisible elements of our imagination, we exercise the muscles needed to crystallize those images.

The Take Away

As children we spend a lot of time using our imaginations to explain the world around us. However, many adults still work hard to use their mind's eye. These conversations should prepare students to draw from their imaginations and intellect in creative ways--today and every day for the rest of their lives.

Teacher Reflection:

Imaginative students need imaginative teachers. An important step in developing this habitude in our students is to embrace our own imaginative potential; allowing ourselves to be creative. The following reflection questions are intended to give you a window into your own creative spirit:

How are you creative?

Do you spend time with other creative people?

Do you play, laugh, and use humor to enhance experiences?

Do you fantasize?

Do you express your own creative talents? Do you paint, cook, sew, write…?

Do you daydream, by just letting your mind wander?

Do you make up similes and metaphors?

Do you pay attention, to small ideas that might someday become big?

Do you take yourself out of your comfort zone?

Final Thoughts:

We tend to think imagination is child's play, yet in reality, every human being has an imagination. It may be repressed, inactive, or distorted, but it exists. When people are asked about their imagination, many may reply they have none, others will claim they have too much. Some might say they lost theirs long ago. When we talk to our students about their imaginations, let's not ask whether they have one (because they do), but rather what are they going to do with it?

Imagination Resources For Students

My Beautiful Child by Lisa Desimini

Mama, if you had a Wish by Jeanne Modesitt

Imagine a Day by Sarah Thomson

Imagine a Night by Rob Gonsalves

Alice the Fairy by David Shannon

It Looks Like Spilt Milk by Charles G. Shaw

Harold and the Purple Crayon by Crockett Johnson

Where the Wild Things Are by Maurice Sendak

Clara and Asha by Eric Rohmann

The Snowy Day by Ezra Jack Keats

Imagine That by Jane Wilson

Imagine by Norman Messenger

The Dot by Peter Reynolds

Museum Trip by Barbara Lehman

My Chair by Betsy James

Picture This: Perception and Composition by Molly Bang

One Red Dot by David Carter

What Does Peace Feel Like? by Vladimir Radunsky

All I See by Cynthia Rylant

Close Your Eyes by Jean Marzollo

Color Me a Rhyme by Jane Yolen

Imagination Resources for Teachers

Buzan's Book of Genius by Tony Buzan and Raymond Keene

Creating Minds by Howard Gardner

Creativity - Beyond the Myth of Genius by Robert Weisberg

The Great Thinkers by Edward de Bono & George Weidenfeld

Image and Brain: The Resolution of the Imagery Debate by Kosslyn, S.M.

How the Mind Works by Pinker

The Matter of Minds by Vendler, Z. 1984.

HABITUDE #1: IMAGINATION

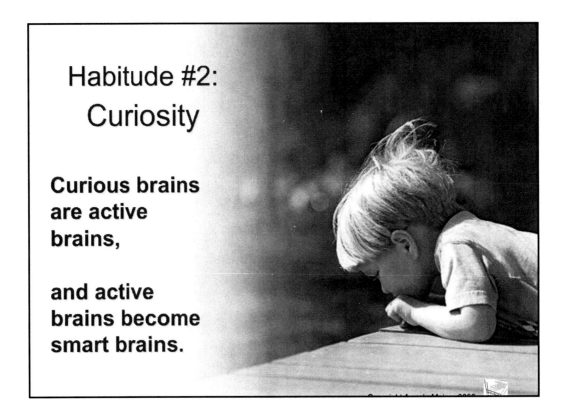

Habitude #2:
Curiosity

**Curious brains
are active
brains,**

**and active
brains become
smart brains.**

Habitude # 2:
Curiosity

"Curiosity is one of the most permanent and certain characteristics of a vigorous intellect." Samuel Johnson, 1751

Who wouldn't want to be without curiosity? Great minds are curious. You would be hard pressed to find an intellectual giant who is not: Thomas Edison; Leonardo da Vinci; Albert Einstein; Richard Feynman; all curious characters. Yet, I wonder...

- How do some students end up more curious than others?

- How can we add curiosity to our teaching toolbox and our conversations regarding teaching and learning?

- How can we live more curious lives ourselves as we model for our students what living a curious life is like?

This chapter seeks to explore the answers to these questions. The lessons that follow will help develop and nurture student's curious instincts as they work consciously on their habitude of curiosity.

Porch Pitch: Why Curiosity Matters

Without a doubt, curiosity is a trait of genius minds, but why is curiosity so important to our students and their learning? Here's my porch pitch:

- Curiosity keeps the brain active and awake

- Curiosity keeps us open and ready for new ideas

- Curiosity keeps life and learning exciting

Questions like "what if" and "I wonder" keep us in motion. Curious brains are active brains and active brains become smart brains. Like any muscle, the mental exercise caused by curiosity makes the mind stronger. Curious people live full and adventurous lives as each new quest and question leads them down roads otherwise not traveled. So let the questions begin!

Million Dollar Conversation Starter (Anchor Lesson):

I want this first conversation with kids to be clear and specific. The teaching point is curiosity.

Good morning boys and girls, our lesson today is about curiosity and the role being curious plays in your learning. So let me ask you this...What does curiosity mean to you?

To keep thinking active and public, I create an anchor chart to record student's thoughts and responses to the question. Kindergartners were eager to share.

- Curiosity means...

- You have to ask a lot of questions

- You are really excited about learning

- You think about stuff you are reading and learning and wonder about it

- You discover answers to things you want to find out more about

- Learning about things you love

- The teacher wonders what you want to know about a topic, and then she puts your questions under the "W" of the chart (KWL strategy)

- Having tons of questions in your brain

- Thinking hard

- I am not exactly sure, but I think it has something to do with school- it could be a good thing?!

When all thoughts of curiosity are captured on the chart, I invite students to hear what others have said about the topic. The conversation continues...

Boys and girls thank you so much for sharing your thoughts and ideas with me. I thought you might be interested in hearing what others have said about curiosity. I have collected several famous quotes about curiosity and the importance of living a curious life. As you work in small groups today, I am going to provide each group with a famous quote and a piece of chart paper to record your thinking on. As you read what these famous voices are saying about curiosity, this is what I want you to consider and respond to:

- How is this person defining curiosity?

- How did curiosity benefit them as a learner?

- What is being said about curiosity that we can apply in our lives?

There are many quotes to choose from that can be collected from any specific field or discipline. Here are just a few to get you started.

- "The desire to know is natural to great men." – Leonardo da Vinci

- "Curiosity is one of the permanent and certain characteristics of a vigorous mind." – Samuel Johnson

- "Judge a man by his questions rather than by his answers."- Voltaire

- "Curiosity is the very basis of education and if you tell me that curiosity killed the cat, I say only the cat died nobly."- Arnold Edinborough

- "The important thing is not to stop questioning. Curiosity has its own reason for existing. One cannot help but be in awe when he contemplates the mysteries of eternity, of life, of the marvelous structure of reality. It is enough if one tries merely to comprehend a little of this mystery every day. Never lose a holy curiosity."- Albert Einstein

- "Wisdom begins in wonder." – Socrates

- "Curiosity must be kept alive. One must never, for whatever reason, turn his back on life." - Eleanor Roosevelt

- "The greatest virtue of man is perhaps curiosity." - Anatole France

- "Curiosity is lying in wait for every secret." - Ralph Waldo Emerson

- "Mere curiosity adds wings to every step." – Goethe

Students write, draw, and discuss their reactions and responses to the quote on their chart paper. Each chart is displayed around the room, creating a "quote wall." Students can travel with group members adding their additional reactions and perspectives to each quote. The conversation culminates with powerful discussion of the value and necessity to tap into and develop their own curiosity Habitude.

These questions facilitate self-reflection and application of our curiosity conversation to their own learning lives.

- What are you most curious about?

- What subjects in school are you most interested in?

- What is it about those subjects that interest you most?

- If you could study or investigate any topic, what would it be?

- How does your curiosity affect how you approach a topic? A text? How hard you may work or how you feel?

Lessons that Last: Continuing the Dialogue

Curiosity cannot be "mastered." It develops over time and with practice. The following curiosity lessons provide you with specific ideas and tools to build curiosity, develop students question asking capabilities, and create opportunities for self-reflection. These lessons do not follow a prescribed scope and sequence. They can and should be expanded and extended over days and weeks. These conversations keep the habitude alive and moving, so students link curiosity in their deskwork and their life work.

Lesson One: Building Curiosity

According to Mikhail Csikszentmihalyi, there is a direct relationship between attention and our interest in the world. In other words, nothing is interesting to us unless we pay attention to it. Rocks are not interesting until we begin collecting them. People in the mall are not interesting until we become curious about their lives. Vacuum cleaners are not interesting until we need a new one. According to Csikszentmihalyi, we can develop our curiosity (and fight boredom) by making a conscious effort to build curiosity by paying attention.

To test his theory in the classroom, I give students the following curiosity challenge:

Think of a topic you have studied or are studying that you believe is the MOST uninteresting. (Apologies to science and math teachers, but some of most immediate responses include: rocks, molecules, and fractions.) The good news is that we can turn uninteresting into interesting, finding relevance in ANY topic if we make a conscious effort to direct our attention and questions toward that topic. Let's see how it goes. Have students pick a subject, focus on curiosity, and turn the subject inside out and upside down.

In Grade 10, here is what happened when we looked at rocks through a curiosity lens:

- How many kinds of rock have been identified?

- What if we could turn all rock into fuel?

- How many uses are there for rock?

- What rock has been the most valuable?

- Who invented that saying, "harder than a rock?"

- How does rock turn into diamonds or other jewels?

- Where can I find the largest rock?

- When climbers climb rock, how do they hold on?

- How many injuries have occurred because of rocks?

- Are there still rock slides in America?

- Has anyone ever died from a rock slide?

- Why is gravel cheap rock?

- Is volcanic rock softer than normal rock?

- When does a rock turn into a mountain?

And through their lens, second-grade students wondered about rocks in this way...

- Do rocks matter to nature or are they just there?

- What is the oldest rock?

- How are rocks formed?

- Are there new kinds of rocks being created today?

- Is there anything in the world that is harder than a rock?

- What make the colors in rocks?

- When rocks form, how long does that take?

- What is the difference between a rock and a mineral?

- Do other planets have rock like Earth?

- What makes some rocks smooth?

- What are the biggest rock collections in the world?

- What is the softest, what is the hardest rock?

- Is a cliff just one big rock?

How about your students? What would their topics be? How would they respond?

After the exercise, it's time to reflect with students about the experience of using curiosity to turn a subject we were not excited about into something worthy of our time and attention:

Boys and Girls, let me ask you this:

- Was being curious worth it?

- In what way did being intentionally curious change how you felt about the topic we were studying?

- Did paying attention in this way make the topic more interesting?

- Did having others around help?

- What challenges still remain?

These questions ignite great conversations about future learning and behavior as not everything we read or learn will be of interest to our brains. Demonstrating to students their own ability to turn the "uninteresting" into the interesting - and yes, even have fun in the process - is invaluable.

Encourage your students to test this theory in other aspects of their lives as well, challenging them to be purposefully curious outside the classroom. So the next time they are at the grocery store, in the car, or even watching TV, encourage them to notice, really notice, and ask questions... just because they can!

Lesson Two: Questions: Tools for Curious Minds

Curiosity fuels our imagination. Our wonderment serves as a prerequisite to the questions we ask. In this lesson, I want students to see how curiosity and questioning go hand-in-hand. The following texts do a great job showing students the way curious minds work by using questions as tools for powerful thinking and learning.

Where Do Balloons Go? by Jamie Lee Curtis works wonderfully for starting this conversation with younger students and Eve Merriam's, *The Wise Woman and Her Secrets* ignites powerful dialogue of older students. Both texts feature a "curious" main character whose wonder about the world sparks in them a plethora of questions.

Before introducing the stories, I ask kids to think about curious people they know or have read about. How do you know they are curious? What about them tells you so?

As students share examples and descriptions of curious people, they will see that a hallmark of curious minds is the capacity and capability to ask lots of questions. As we explore the characters in the text, I encourage students to look for evidence that the main character is curious or exhibits curious behavior. Students see that curious characters, both in books and in life, use questions to awaken, explore, and sustain their curiosity.

To applaud and practice asking questions as a way to embrace and enhance curiosity, I ask students to collect the questions that are most important to them in a special box or container. These "Wonder Boxes" (Debbie Miller, 2002) help students initiate and track their inquiries about topics they are passionate and curious about.

Students are given the opportunity to explore these topics and questions in their reading and learning, and from time to time I am able to take them though the entire inquiry cycle demonstrating how expert learners are able to find answers to questions they feel most curious and convicted about.

Lesson Three: Albert Knows Best: Asking Genius Questions

Our students start life like Einstein with curiosity and an insatiable desire to learn. As time goes on, students grow to believe that answers are more important than the questions. This lesson puts the emphasis and importance back on the question asking.

Boys and girls,

Do you agree with the following statement: Thinking is a process of asking and answering questions? (Say yes?!?) If we want to change the quality of our thinking, then we must look carefully at the kinds of questions we are asking.

One of the most powerful thinkers in history was Albert Einstein. He was not only passionately curious, but he knew the importance of asking powerful questions. What made Albert stand out were the kinds of questions he asked. He did not just look at a problem or a text and ask who, what, where, when and how. Albert's questions were different...and numerous.

Now, here is the good news. The power to think at this high level is not just reserved for genius minds. We can learn from Albert. Today we are going to practice "Thinking like Albert" using his questioning state of mind to help us explore our topic. We are going to practice asking one another genius level questions. To help us, I've created a deck of question cards. I call them Q-cards. The Q-cards have questions that Albert and other genius minds might ask if they were here exploring this topic with us.

We will use the Q- cards to help us as we explore _____ (ex. transportation) today. The most important thing about this exercise is to keep asking questions. Do not worry about finding the answers, just keep asking. Our brains have Einstein power, are we ready to use them wisely? Let's make Albert proud.

I want students to leave this experience reflecting on the following:

- Which question asked was most genius?

- Which question are you most proud of?

- What kind of questions did you hear yourself asking often?

- What is another question you might now ask yourself?

This lesson works well when I divide students into small groups, giving their own deck of genius questions. (See Appendix) As they practice "thinking like Albert," I walk around and listen in, complimenting, coaching, and giving them feedback. Remember, even Albert did not become genius overnight. With time and practice, students will become more skilled and confident question-askers.

Lesson Four: The right question at the right time

How often have we heard this: So, Mrs. Maiers, what is the right answer?"

The following conversation tries to move students toward asking this instead, "Mrs. Maiers, do you think I have the right question?"

The ability to ask the right kind of question, at the right time is the hallmark of a truly efficient and successful learner. Like drivers in a car, the right question can plow the road ahead or leave us stuck in a ditch along the side of the highway. Being in charge of the questions we ask matters. Successful thinking and learning require questions to be framed in a wide variety of ways. The "framing" of our questions dramatically influences what we can and are able to understand. Just teaching students to question is not enough. It is critical to explore where different questions take us as learners.

Boys and Girls, we have been talking a great deal lately about the importance of curiosity and asking powerful questions. I want to share with you a quote that I came across that will help us think about our work today as learners:

Einstein once remarked that if he were about to be killed and had only one hour to figure out how to save his life, he would devote the first 55 minutes of that hour to searching for the right question. Once he had that question, Einstein said, finding the answer would take only about 5 minutes.

As learners, when we get to the point where we know what kind of question to ask, we are in a much better position to understand what we are reading and learning about. I want to share with you how different questions get us to different places. An "I wonder?" question leads us in a different direction than a "How is it like?" question. It is important for us to know how the types of questions we ask impact and influence the answers we are capable of getting. Over the next weeks, we are going to explore many kinds or types of questions together: (Adapted from the work of Jamie McKenzie)

- Clarifying Questions

- Sorting and Sifting Out Questions

- Strategic Questions

- Planning Questions

- Elaboration Questions

- Comparing Questions

I want students to see that each type of question is a tool in their thinking toolbox. A variety of "tools" may be needed to complete a project, and those tools must be chosen carefully.

This is a challenge for many students who have never thought consciously about how they think or question. Thinking tools lie unsorted, unlabeled, and unidentifiable in the bottom of their box. They tend to reach into the box and pull out the first tool (or question) that comes to hand (or mind). This leads to hammering when drilling is needed instead.

To introduce students to the idea of categorizing questions, I suggest bringing in a toolbox of tools. Talk to students about how they might be organized in the toolbox based on what they do. This is the same sorting and labeling process that can be used to explore questions we ask in reading and learning. Before long students can reach into their "questioning tool box" and consciously select the question needed as meaning is revealed, reflected upon, and responded to.

Lesson Five: Becoming a Curious Reader

When I was ten years old, I wanted to be Nancy Drew. She taught me that things were not always as they seem and that mysteries were meant to be solved. Her chief strength as a detective was her curiosity. Her questions emulated her dissatisfaction with easy answers. This is this same passionate curiosity I want for my readers. I teach them to enter each text and task with the same fever and purpose that detectives use to solve their mysteries. Great reading is about excavating, uncovering, and discovering meaning. Like Nancy, curious readers are never satisfied with easy answers.

Becoming a curious reader means explicitly teaching students to think and act like detectives. Great reading, like detective work, is grounded in questions: questions of the text and content, of the writer, and of themselves. Introduce students to the idea that reading is like being a detective. Detectives do not just enter a crime scene and ask questions. They ask questions as a matter of learning how to work through the process of reading. They go beyond the questions raised during a first reading to begin seeing the complex patterns and interpretive gaps, which make reading exciting and challenging.

The Take Away

By the end of the habitude study, here are the things I want students to take away from our conversations around curiosity.

1. Be courageous with your questions: Lots of people saw apples fall, but only Sir Isaac Newton dared ask how or why. Someone smarter than me once said, "Ask the question, play the fool; don't ask the question, stay the fool." The only dumb question is the one not asked.

2. Questions help us: Questions allow us to make sense of the world. They are the most powerful tools we have for making decisions and solving problems, for inventing, changing and improving our lives as well as the lives of others. Questioning is central to learning and growing.

3. Being curious is a FUN way to be: Happy people ask lots of questions. We grew up thinking that, "curiosity killed the cat." To the contrary, it was curiosity that gave the cat nine lives. Curious learners are happy learners. It is easy to find life fascinating and to begin wondering "why?" and "how?"

4. And most importantly this: Questions, not answers define you as a learner.

Celebrate when your students ask "Why is the sky blue?", "Who made clouds?", or "What happens if...?" Let students know that their questions matter. The smartest students become the one who asks the wisest questions.

Reflection:

We must be the curious learners we wish our students to be. The following questions are intended to help us, model, demonstrate, and share our own curious learning lives:

- How are you curious?

- When was the last time that you sought knowledge simply for the pursuit?

- How was your life enriched by curiosity?

- What is the role of curiosity in your classroom?

- How curious are your students?

- When is the last time your students were allowed to seek knowledge in a topic that they were curious about?

- What have you done in your classroom environment to enrich and support curiosity to develop?

Final Thoughts

I think, at a child's birth, if a mother could ask a fairy godmother to endow it with the most useful gift, that gift would be curiosity. -Eleanor Roosevelt

Like parents, holding a newborn infant, we can feel overwhelmed by an awesome sense of responsibility for shaping young lives and minds. If our classrooms remain places where curiosity is nurtured, developed, and celebrated, the gift we give students extends far beyond our classroom walls.

Curiosity Resources for Students

Curious George Books by H.A. Rey

Miss Maggie by Cynthia Rylant

Nope, What If, and A Light in the Attic by Shel Silverstein

Un-Brella by Scott E. Franson

Two Bad Ants by Chris Van Allsburg

Picturescape by Elisa Gutierrez

Sector 7 by David Wiesner

Zoom by Istvan Banyai

ReZoom by Istvan Banyai

Exploring the Unexplained by Kelly Knauer

The Three Questions by Jon Muth

The Wise Woman and Her Secret by Eve Merriam

Where Do Balloons Go? by Jamie Lee Curtis

A Time of Wonder by Robery McCloskey

The Stranger by Chris Van Allsburg

The Mysteries of Harris Burdock by Chris Ban Allsburg

How Come? by Kathy Wollard

The Hidden Alphabet by Laura Seeger

Curiosity Resources For Teachers

Developing More Curious Minds by Barell, John

Strategies that Work. Harvey, Stephanie and Goudvis, Anne.

Build Your Own Information Literate School. Koechlin, Carol and Sandi Zwaan.

Info Tasks for Successful Learning. Koechlin, Carol and Sandi Zwaan.

Teaching Tools for the Information Age. Koechlin, Carol and Sandi Zwaan.

Learning to Question to Wonder to Learn. McKenzie, Jamie.

Asking Better Questions. Morgan, Norah.

Habitude #3:
Perseverance

Perseverance
is not only the
ability to get done
what needs to
be done --

but to continue
the effort no
matter what.

HABITUDE 3: PERSEVERANCE

"Nobody trips over mountains. It is the small pebble that causes you to stumble. Pass all the pebbles in your path and you will find you have crossed the mountain."
~Author Unknown

Recently, I cleared a mountain. I completed running in my first half-marathon. Physically and mentally the critical aspects of perseverance came to life. Just one year prior, I had never run a mile, let alone completed a marathon. It was just too big a mountain. As our training team reflected on this experience, we agreed our turning point came when we stopped trying to climb the mountain (run the marathon) and began concentrating on the pebbles; our day to day commitment to running. Once we knew we could endure rain, snow, lack of sleep, and apathy, we realized we were champions before we stepped one foot into the race. We lived the habitude of perseverance.

It was this experience that helped me unpack what I think I've always known but rarely articulated about perseverance. Success is not always about the mountains we climb, but rather our ability to handle the pebbles in our pathway. Our "running stories," those stories of perseverance should be shared in every classroom.

Porch Pitch: Why Perseverance Matters

Perseverance is the cornerstone of any successful endeavor, in school and out. It is a key to victory over unfavorable circumstances.

A student's ability to perform and commit to excellence requires:

- Preparedness with clear goals in sight

- Courageous Conviction

- Self-Management

- Dreaming big with passion fueling the way

The following lessons and conversations will help students build their perseverance muscles as they train like intellectual athletes.

Million Dollar Conversation (Anchor Lesson):

What is perseverance? How do I recognize it? Do I have it?

My goal for this first conversation is to answer these questions. Here's how we start:

I place a newly wrapped toy in front of the group, one preferably difficult to open (the more like Ft. Knox, the better). Make sure your "toy" is appropriate to the grade level in both enticement and difficulty. Give students adequate time to struggle opening the package. After the students get the package open (or not), maybe after several minutes, I turn to the board and write this definition: "Perseverance: The act of continuing to do something in spite of difficulty or opposition."

As we reflect on this experience, I have students discuss the following:

- What kept you from throwing the toy across the room when you got frustrated?

- What were you saying to yourself? What made you keep you trying?

- How did others help? How did they hinder?

From our toy experiment, students recognize that someone has persevered when we observe:

- Commitment, hard work, patience, and endurance

- Ability to handle difficulty calmly and without complaint

- Trying again and again

- Acceptance of support and encouragement within one's self or others

This is a great time to share the timeless story of the *Little Engine That Could*, a perfect example of these principals in action. (Any story illustrating the Habitude can be substituted.)

In small groups, students are asked to give specific examples of how they demonstrated perseverance in our toy experience. I move the discussion into their learning lives, by providing examples of when these habits are present in the classroom.

Boys and Girls, you show me you are persevering when you:

- Give up your TV time to spend hours studying

- Try a new assignment that is difficult without giving up

- Have a problem but keep on studying even when discouraged

- Come to school after a hard night and still try your best

- Miss a day of school but work hard to catch up

- Are at the end of a difficult race but you still cross the finish line

- Try out for something again, even if you weren't successful the first time

A great follow up to this discussion is the book, I Knew I Could by Craig Forman. I want students to know they have persevered in some way, and they can and must continue to do so in order to be successful. For deeper reflection, I have students complete these two sentences:

I show perseverance when...

I know it because I...

Lessons that Last: Continuing the Dialogue

Perseverance cannot be "mastered." It develops over time and with practice. The following perseverance lessons provide you with specific ideas and tools to build perseverance. These lessons do not follow a prescribed scope and sequence. They can and should be, expanded and extended over days and weeks. These conversations keep the habitude alive and moving so students link perseverance in their deskwork and their life work.

Lesson One: Life Happens

Perseverance is not only the ability to get done what needs to be done, but to continue the effort no matter what.

When I think of people that have achieved their goals while enduring incredible obstacles, and I think of Abraham Lincoln overcoming the lack of formal education. I think of Gandhi and Martin Luther King who both overcame hatred and prejudice. Viktor Frankl was able to survive the brutality of Nazi concentration camps and the loss of all that was dear to him. The list can go on and on of incredible achievements of valor, glory, and fame. The point I really want to make is how perseverance is not a magical quality but a mindset -- an attitude -- of how we view the obstacles we face in life.

Persevering through a task is easy to do when nothing gets in the way. But, how often does that happen? It's the no-matter-what part of the habitude where difficulty lies. We all know that things get in the way and that life can be hard, right? Real perseverance happens when you do it anyway, in spite of opposition.

I begin this lesson with an exploration of famous individuals and their success stories. As we look upon some great historical figures, we find many of them persevered against tremendous odds. Though we admire their accomplishments, the focus of this conversation is the enduring qualities that allowed them to find success in life.

The following are examples of perseverance preceding triumph:

Beethoven (composer) – deaf

Ray Charles (musician) - blind

Thomas Edison (inventor) - learning problems

Albert Einstein (scientist) - learning disability

Helen Keller (author) - deaf and blind

Franklin D. Roosevelt (president) - paralyzed from polio

Vincent Van Gogh (artist) - mentally ill

Christopher Reeves (actor) - Paralyzed from an accident

For many people, sickness, disability, and adversity would have been nothing more than a tragedy. Each one of these individuals became better, not bitter because of it.

I want students to understand that these remarkable people are examples of how to act when adversity or tragedy enters life.

Students can brainstorm ways that they can behave in the face of adversity. Many responses can get personal, but it's important to, in some way, make public their accomplishments. I take note when I see students:

- Face and accept what happens to them

- Express and talk about the feelings they are having

- Get help and support of others

- Learn and grow from the experience, even when it hurts

- Try to make a situation better

I want students to understand that people aren't able to persevere because they are famous or successful, though their success and fame are due in large part to their ability to persevere.

Lesson Two: Failing To Succeed

Persevering learners view failure as a learning experience, using each mistake as tuition, and each situation as an opportunity to glean something new. Stories of individuals overcoming the odds are inspiration to all, but the heart of perseverance, and the reason a very small percentage of people ever achieve their full potential is they give up after the first sign of struggle. The phrase "try, try again" is not just fodder for encouragement, but are the reason so few achieve if they don't hear that clarion call. It is estimated that 90 percent of people gave up just about the time they were ready to succeed. If they had only kept on going...

To illustrate this point, I give students the following "Success Quiz" (See Appendix for handout). As I read the statements about each of these true-life persons, students decide whether or not the person was a success or failure in their field. Go ahead-give it a try yourself, and feel free to add others, famous or not, to the list.

SUCCESS OR FAILURE?

_____ Artist: All he wanted to do was to sketch cartoons. He applied with a Kansas City newspaper. The editor said, "It's easy to see from these sketches that you have no talent." No studio would give him a job. He ended up doing publicity work for a church in an old, dilapidated garage.

_____ Writer: Living in a car, trying to make ends meet, this writer submitted her first children's book to 27 publishers. She was rejected each time.

_____ Athlete: As a baseball player, he once held the record for striking out more than any player in the history of baseball: 1,330 times.

_____ Politician: defeated 7 times in run for political office.

_____ Athlete: missed his target 9,000 times, lost 300 games

So, what were your answers? Whether you answered success or failure, you're right! Each of these people was both a failure and success. Here's a bit of the conversation that follows:

Boys and Girls,

Let me ask you this, would you have kept on playing baseball if you struck out 1,330 times? Babe Ruth did and wound up with 714 home runs. Would you have kept on in politics if you were defeated 7 times? I am so glad that Abraham Lincoln didn't. Would you have given up on the third time, fourth, sixth? Abe hung in there and succeeded in becoming the 16th and one of the most respected, presidents of the United States.

And what about the cartoonist whom no one would hire? The one who was told that he had no talent? The old garage he worked in was in such bad shape that it had mice. One day, he sketched one of those mice. Any guesses as to the name of that mouse? The mouse one day became famous as "Mickey Mouse." The artist, of course, was Walt Disney. The writer whose children's book was rejected by 23 publishers? Take a wild guess. Dr. Seuss. By the way, the 24th publisher sold six million copies.

And NBA great, Michael Jordan once said, "I have missed more that 9,000 shots in my career. I have lost almost 300 games. On 26 occasions, I have been entrusted with

the game winning shot...and I missed. I have failed over and over and over again in my life. And that is precisely why I succeed."

Successful people never give in. They just keep on going and going, and here is why: Failure is a part of success. Successful people expect to fail.

You cannot choose when success is going to be, so you have to keep on going, keep on giving, and keep on practicing, so you will be ready for that moment when it comes.

These are great points to ponder as lead perfectly into our next discussion; failure-our best teacher!

Lesson Three: Failure – Our Best Teacher

Failure is an important aspect of all that we do in education. It is a big part of the process that helps stimulate and cement learning. Yet, our educational system is and continues to be fixated on "right answers." Not embracing failure is enormously deceiving to students and builds resistance and fear into our students' perceptions of failure. Ultimately, it paralyzes students from asking questions and attempting to answer them for fear of failure. Students learn the lesson of "right" and so they fear failure and see it as the enemy of their potential success.

This lesson explores failure in a new light. My goal in this lesson is for students not only to expect failure and see it as an opportunity to learn, but to discuss productive ways to handle failure and persevere. I want students to practice developing success from failures.

After giving each student a piece of paper and some colored pencils or markers, I let them know I will be revealing a word that is an important part of being able to persevere. The word is so important that I want to do more than just discuss its meaning; I then want to capture their thoughts and feelings about the word on paper. I reveal the word FAILURE in large black, bold letters on the board. I use the following prompts to help them explore their associations with failure:

- What experience comes to you most?

- What do you remember about failing at something?

- What words come to mind when you hear "FAILIURE"?

- What color is failure?

- What feelings are strongest?

Before sharing in a large group, students meet in small groups to discuss their word sketches. I ask one student to report back to the group general feelings and observations, so that none of the students has to share a negative experience.

As you can imagine, students detest and fear failure. In some manner, so do adults, yes? That's where our "running stories" come in. Here's an example:

Boys and Girls,

For the last week, I have recorded things both in school and out that have not gone as planned. I failed at achieving my goal.

- Wanted to exercise at least 4 times

- I wanted to have my lessons plans done

- I did not spend as much time with my family as I should have

- I tried a new recipe and my family hated it

Here is the good news, look at all the lessons I have learned this week: I am now able to have a much better week because I have learned from my mistakes. I am in a position to make wiser choices about my behavior and time. It is okay to feel disappointed, but my excitement for the week ahead of me overrides that!

As you persist towards your goals this week, you will fail. Failure is not your enemy, perfection is. Not doing something because of fear or perfection is failure. Trying, failing, getting up...that is success!

Here is what I would like you to do for the next week. I want you to keep a journal of the times you have experienced frustration or failure. I want you to record every one, even if it seems small; I want you to write that down. At the end of the week, we are going to record those examples on this chart, but right next to the failure, we are going to find one positive thing that resulted from our failure.

Lesson Four: Slow And Steady

"Success isn't something you chase. It's something you have to put forth the effort for constantly. Then maybe it'll come when you least expect it. Most people don't understand that."– Michael Jordan

A conversation about persistence would not be complete without our friends, Tortoise and Hare. Anyone who remembers Aesop's famous fable will recall that the wise tortoise knew he must work hard to beat the speedy hare, and his persistence was what won him the prize.

In our fast paced world, where gratification is instant, slow and steady is a hard sell. It is easy to repeat the error the rabbit made, and wish for -- possibly create -- shortcuts. The challenge in reaching any meaningful goal requires persistence. It's persistence that keeps us moving forward. Meaningful goals are not achieved overnight. They require – no they demand – persistence, patience, and perseverance. If you continue to take action, you will build the necessary momentum.

I saved this fable for our last conversation because it reflects the essence of all our conversations. First, we learn the value of perseverance as slow and steady wins the race. Secondly, we learn that achieving any goal in life requires hard work, even when we feel like giving up or giving in. Finally, this tale illustrates that success can be achieved against all odds. The impossible becomes possible if we don't give up.

Take Away:

As I wrote this chapter, I envisioned the faces of my students who had a tough time academically. For some, life at home was in shambles, and I know they come to school wondering if they would ever make it through school, sometimes a school day. I want students walking away with one big idea: they are stronger than they think they are. If I can help them find a goal, however small, that is worth enduring, they can experience in my classroom their abilities to clear the pebbles, and by doing that, cross the mountain.

Final Thoughts:

Students will respect you for your successes, but they will love you when you're vulnerable about your struggles through hard times. Your stories will add credence to the message that can do attitudes are not just encouraging words in stories. Whether you are running a race, or working through a difficult problem in school, perseverance is the difference between success and failure.

Resources:

Primary Resources:

Tortoise and the Hare Aesop's Fables

The Carrot Seed by Ruth Krauss

John Henry by Julius Lester

The Little Engine That Could by Watty Piper

Mirette on the High Wire by Arnold McCully

Wilma Unlimited by Kathleen Krull

Alexander and the Terrible, No Good, Very Bad Day by Judith Viorst

A Chair for My Mother by Vera Williams

How Many Days to America? by Eve Bunting

The Little Red Ant and the Great Big Crumb by Shirley Climo

Pancakes for Breakfast by Tomie De Paola

The Little Red Hen by Paul Galdone

Snowflake Bentley by Jacqueline Briggs Martin

D.W. Flips by Marc Brown

Intermediate Resources:

The Big Wave by Pearl S. Buck

The Book of Virtues by William Bennett

Call It Courage by Armstrong Sperry

The Diary of a Young Girl by Anne Frank

Island of the Blue Dolphins by Scott O'Dell

Julie of the Wolves by Jean Craighead George

Nothing Is Impossible by Dorothy Aldis

Sadako and the Thousand Paper Cranes by Eleanor Coerr

Sarah Plain and Tall by Patricia MacLachlan

Stone Fox by John Reynolds Gardiner

Reach Higher by Scottie Pippen

Wizards Hall by Jane Yolen

Holes by Louis Sachar

Hatchet by Gary Paulsen

Sky Pioneer: a Photobiography of Amelia Earhart by Corinne Szabo

Habitude #4:
Self Awareness

Self Awareness
is the ability to
think and exist
inside --

and outside
of ourselves
simultaneously.

HABITUDE # 4:
SELF-AWARENESS

Knowing others is wisdom, knowing yourself is Enlightenment."- Tao Tzu

As lifelong learners, our growth should never cease. Part of our growth is improving our understanding of self - why we feel what we feel, why we behave how we behave. This understanding affords us opportunity and independence in changing ourselves, allowing us to create the life we desire. Yet, without fully knowing ourselves - who we are, what we believe, why we make certain choices - self acceptance and change are all the more difficult.

The quest towards self knowledge goes beyond articulating what we want from life or who we want to become. Self-Awareness is the ability to simultaneously exist both inside and outside of ourselves. It's with this intimate knowledge we're equipped to make conscious and deliberate decisions about the course we wish our lives to take; not just retrospectively, but proactively.

The habitude of self-awareness acts as our own built in check-and-balance system, popping up when there are conflicts that exist between our true nature and what we are actually doing or thinking. We may not always know how to reach our destination, and may from time to time become lost, but at the very least, we'll understand when we're off track and be able to search mindfully for a new route.

Helping our students recognize how self awareness can both guide and empower is what makes this a habitude worth the study.

Porch Pitch: Why Awareness Matters in Learning

Knowing who you are, where you are going and what you want to be when you grow up is an obvious benefit in your life's quest, but what about self awareness as it pertains to learning? Is the quest to know yourself as a learner equally beneficial? The answer is unequivocally, yes.

Champion learners:

- Recognize their strengths and weaknesses making them more able to match their abilities to specific situations and settings

- Are self driven, they set goals, make plans, and learn with purpose and passion

- Monitor their behaviors, actions, and thinking to ensure they are staying on track towards their goals

- Are more confident and successful. They know what they are doing, and what it takes to get there

- Are efficient and able to make clear decisions about the best way to apply strategies and techniques to further their goals

Far too often, students see learning as something done to them. They look for solutions to their challenges outside of themselves - in teachers; in books; in classmates. Students leave our classrooms with answers about a lot of stuff, but with too many questions about themselves: How will I handle a challenge? Do I have the strategies it takes? What gifts do I bring to the world? Can their gifts help them engage in the world?

The following lessons and conversations are intended to help students to become experts about themselves so they learn how to make the best use of their abilities, skills, and talents. Combined with smart teaching, it is a win-win for all!

Million Dollar Conversation (Anchor Lesson):

Good Morning Boys and Girls,

When I talk to you about learning, many times our conversations are about what we are learning or what I want you to know or do. Today's conversation is all about you and who you are as learners. This is a conversation about the habitude of self-awareness. Successful learning involves more than just knowledge of the content - it involves knowledge of yourself as a learner.

Self-Aware learners know how they learn best. They are able to recognize their strengths and weaknesses, and most importantly are able to monitor and control their own learning process. In this way, learning success in not up to someone else, it is something I want you to be in charge of for yourself. It is what I want most for you, to feel confident and in charge of your own learning. Becoming self aware is the first step to getting you there. So, let's get to know ourselves, shall we?

I want to be clear. There is no right or wrong way to learn. Just like fingerprints, every learner is different and therefore has different needs to make learning successful. Some learners work better by themselves in a quiet room, others need people around to keep them focused and motivated. Each and every one of you has a unique learner personality. You each have different strengths, different challenges. The goal of our lesson today is for you to recognize what your strengths and challenges are so you can figure out how you work and learn best.

Here's what I would like you to do. Close your eyes and think about a learning experience that was very positive for you; one you learned a lot from or were successful in doing. It can be anything from tying your shoes to learning how to swim. It does not have to be learning that happened in school. After the image is clear in your mind, I want you to take a few minutes and draw or sketch what is happening. Jot down some words or ideas that come to mind about the experience. As we share, I am going to ask you some questions, to help you pinpoint specific things important to you as a learner.

I use the following questions to excavate the specific conditions and characteristics of students learning styles and preferences. These questions can be easily adapted across both grade level and content areas.

- What did you learn most recently?

- Why did you want to learn this? What was your purpose for learning?

- Was your learning motivated by curiosity or necessity?

- How did the learning happen: By doing, watching, or studying?

- Who else was involved in the learning process? How did they help or hinder?

- Where did the learning take place? Did you like that place?

- How did you know you were successful?

- Would you have liked anything to go differently?

The second day the process is repeated by reflecting in the same way, but this time, with an unsuccessful or difficult learning experience.

I culminate the conversations by having students share their reflections and discoveries. They are given the task of creating a learner profile that begins with these two questions:

- I am the sort of person who learns well when...

- I am the sort of person who does not learn well when...

The learner profile can be expanded and entered into a learner portfolio. This is an easy practical tool that provides students with a place to record and reflect on themselves as learners. Even young students are capable of setting learning goals and charting their accomplishments. When students are encouraged to compile artifacts and record their progress during the year, they are able to take ownership of their learning.

Here are some suggested items that could be a part of the Learning Portfolio:

1. A Learner Profile (Created from the questions above)

2. Strengths Assessment (See Appendix) This is a practical tool that records students proclaimed strengths and challenges as a learner

3. Goal Sheet to develop the student's ability to maximize their strengths and strategies they will work on to combat their weaknesses

4. Evidence samples of reading and writing work which reflects the application of the strategies students are working on

5. Self selected highlights that students have chosen to highlight something they have worked hard to accomplish

6. Samples that provide evidence of reading and thinking strategies that have successfully transferred to other subject (i.e., a math or science journal)

*Teachers should consider making contributions to the portfolio; making specific observations we have on our students' skills and abilities.

For our learners to become self aware, and ultimately more effective, these beginning conversations are critical. With knowledge of their learning strengths and preferences, students are well on their way to being the independent, thoughtful, and self-directed learners we desire.

Lessons that Last: Continuing the Dialogue

Self-Awareness cannot be "mastered." It develops over time and with practice. The following self-awareness lessons provide you with specific ideas and tools to build self-awareness. These lessons do not follow a prescribed scope and sequence. They can and should be expanded and extended over days and weeks. These conversations keep the habitude alive and moving, so students link self-awareness in their deskwork and their life work.

Lesson One: Self awareness and Meta-cognition

"Thinking about thinking is the hardest kind of thinking we do!" Olivia - 1st grade student

Meta-cognition is a state of awareness about one's thinking or as Olivia so articulately stated: Meta-cognition is "thinking about thinking."And yes, she is dead on. It is the hardest thinking that we do as learners.

Meta-cognition is difficult to teach, not because our kids do not think, (although they have been accused of that a time or two) but it is difficult to conceptualize because thinking is invisible. You can't see it, you can't touch it, and you can't often hear it. How then, do we go about helping students take control of and manage their thinking?

It all begins with awareness. The kind of awareness that I am striving for in these conversations with students moves beyond who they are as learners, what they like, dislike, etc. into what they do as learners to get the work done.

I refer to this stage of awareness as meta-awareness as it requires learners to be aware of, talk about, think about, and take action on the complex processes involved in learning. This is not something that can be taught in a series of discrete lessons, but has to permeate all lessons and learning conversations; drawing attention to how we use strategies to learn and accomplish tasks. As in this example:

Boys and Girls,

We have been working hard studying _____. What I would like us to talk about is the way we were able to find that solution. What were the strategies that helped us most? Where did the frustration occur, and how did we work through those challenges? If we could talk that out together, even write out a few of our best strategies, I know that will help us the next time we encounter a problem like this. Each day, we are going to build time in to add to our strategy chart because the more we understand the strategies and techniques we use, the more efficient we are the next time around. We have a lot we can learn from one another to improve our performance.

As we ask students to "take their thinking out," examine it, rearrange it and put it back for smarter application, the following sequence of questions guide awareness from simple description of thinking to complex analysis and evaluation.

Step One: Describe Your Thinking

- What kind of thinking did you do?

- What do you call this kind of thinking?

- Can you name this kind of thinking?

- How did it help you find out/solve the problem?'

- 'What was special (or mathematical / scientific / historical etc) about your thinking?'

Step Two: Reflect on Your Thinking

- What did you notice about your thinking?

- What words would you use to describe your thinking?

- How did you do this thinking?

- What did you think about? Why?

- Did you have a plan (or strategy)?

Step Three: Evaluate Your Thinking

- Did you have a good plan (or strategy)?

- Was your thinking good? Why?

- Would you describe your thinking as efficient and effective?

- How could you improve your thinking next time?

Adapted from Schwartz & Parks (1994)

Lesson Two: Champion Readers Are Self Aware

I can remember vividly the days when students looked up at me after finishing a story, and the first question out of my mouth would be —What happened?

After years of asking kids to recall three events, define the bold words, or recite facts, I am thrilled to say that I have evolved. Now, I ask: What are you thinking?

I spent the last several years studying and investigating the thinking that goes on in the minds of proficient readers and learners, so I could give my students the language necessary to talk explicitly about their thinking and the strategies that help them most.

Once students became aware of strategies like schema, inferring and synthesizing, the next challenge became one of application -- the when, where, and how. To bridge this gap between strategy awareness and strategy application, conversations like the following were necessary:

Readers, we have been talking a great deal about the reading and thinking tool of inference. We know that readers who infer act like detectives at a crime scene, looking for critical clues, analyzing those clues, and using the knowledge the author provides to draw logical conclusions.

In today's lesson on making inferences, I want you to watch me as I look for clues about how a character feels and how those clues are different from the traits of the character. Both require the strategy of inference, but the work to figure out a trait vs. a feeling is different. Our goal is to become the kind of reading detective that can infer in any book we pick up.

Thinking aloud like this proves to be the most efficient and effective way to develop meta-awareness in students. Students gradually internalize the dialogue they hear from me so it becomes their inner speech. This awareness allows them to direct their behaviors as they explore their own reading and thinking as authors, mathematicians, or scientists. Over time, they develop into reflective, meta-cognitive, independent learners -- an invaluable step.

"What are you thinking now?" is not only the best question I ask, but the answers I get are extraordinary!

Lesson Three: Hearing Voices-When It is a Good Thing

Champion readers hear voices, and yes, it is a very good thing. The mental dialogues we have with ourselves shape our thinking as we read and learn.

- Wow, look at that!

- Slow down!

- Hmmm, that does not make sense!

- Let me go back and try that again.

- Never knew that!

To give students the experience of that inner conversation, I have adapted this wonderful analogy from the work of Doug Buel:

Readers, today I want you to imagine yourself sitting on a seat in the middle of a bus with a book (or laptop) in your hands. You are trying to read, but you are also continuously distracted. You find yourself looking out the window, watching people get on and off the bus, listening to the wind come through the windows. You notice that sometimes what you are reading makes sense, and at other times your eyes are just looking at the words, and you haven't a clue what you just read.

Now imagine your twin, your aware self occupying the bus seat right next to you. As you've been reading and losing your train of thought, you realize that your aware self has been sitting behind you and noticing everything. Nothing has escaped your aware self: every time your attention has wandered, every time you have just read words and not made sense, your aware self pokes you in the back and whispers in your ear what you should do instead to get you back on track and focused.

How you talk to yourself when you read matters. Think about what the "voice in your head" is telling you. This is the voice of your aware self. Listen carefully as it guides you towards meaning.

When we share our aware self out loud in front of students, we will all soon agree that hearing voices in our heads as readers is a great thing.

Lesson Four: Houston, We Have a Problem

The inner commands or voices we hear have the power to both engage and distract. It is critical for students to become aware and in control of the reading processes as even champion readers engage in "inner conversations" that sometimes lead them astray and far from meaning. It is important for students to realize that our minds lapse into daydreaming or dwell on personal issues that intrude, especially if the reader finds a subject uninteresting or an author boring.

Readers may also become waylaid by struggles with difficult language or challenging ideas.

The following think aloud helps students manage both the engaging and distracting voice (Tovanni, 2000).

Boys and Girls, as I read there is silent conversation going on. In my head, I hear a voice reading the words. It lets me know if I am reciting the words accurately and that they sound like I am talking aloud and not robotic. But another voice I am aware of and attend to is the voice that talks to and interacts with the writer. This is the voice that helps me understand the words I hear myself reciting. I call that my conversation voice, because it is like I am having the conversation with the author as if they were sitting right in the room with me. Thinking about the writer in this way, as if they were in the room, helps me interact with the ideas in the book. Let me show you what I mean...

Last night, I was reading a book by one of my favorite authors, Tomie De Paola called "Now One Foot, Now the Other". In the story, the main character has a relative get sick. My conversation voice was sad because I thought about the time I found out my grandfather had just had a stroke. I remembered those feelings and found it very easy to connect to the character, Bobby, as he was wrestling with those same worries. Along with these thoughts came my memory pictures of my grandfather and me as we played games, sang funny songs, and went on special trips together. Then I started to wonder if Tomie De Paola had experienced illness with someone in his family as I know authors write about things in their own lives. Even days later, the ideas in the text were still with me. When I'm talking back to the text and getting pictures in my mind, I remember more — I understand more.

Ask students to describe times when they have heard their interacting voice? What was the conversation with the writer like?

My goal for the second session was to model how your conversation voice can also lead you astray. Tovani referred to this as the distracting voice. Again I read from Now One Foot, Now the Other:

As I read, "Bobby and his grandfather watched the fireworks." I started to remember the first time I took my kids to see fireworks. My daughter Abby was really scared-she jumped every time there was a pop. Did you catch how my mind started to wander? That was my distracting voice.

I explain to students that connections to the text are very important to help understand and remember what you are reading, but you have to be careful with them. Sometimes one thought will lead to another, and before you know it, you're thinking about something else. That's the distracting voice; the one that leads you away from the text.

Over the next several sessions with students, brainstorm ways to reel the distracting voice in and re-engage with the text. Examples might include:

- Reading slower

- Re-reading

- Pausing and asking a question

- Creating a picture in your mind

How about you? How do you re-engage with the text? Share your strategies and techniques with students often.

Take Away:

Successful learning is not about getting things done, but rather knowing how you got it done, so that you can do it again later, better.

- The two questions I want them walking away everyday wondering:

- What did I learn about myself as a reader/writer/learner today?

- What did I learn that I can do again and again and again?

Final Reflection:

We shower children with awards and recognition because we hope to build confidence. This reinforcement is external and temporary. Confidence comes from within. It is a byproduct of self awareness, a result of knowing our strengths and weaknesses. Self awareness comes from success and failure, independently achieved. There are no awards for self awareness, but it engenders strength of character. Better to nurture this in children than to fill their cabinets full with awards and trophies.

Teacher Reflection:

To help students better understand themselves, we can be the model of how self awareness has influenced our actions and behaviors. Use the following questions as the starting point for your conversations with students. Think about the questions carefully, before formulating your answers.

- Who am I as a reader/learner?

- Can you describe your learning style?

- What do I see myself accomplishing in the next 5 years, 10 years?

- What steps have you taken toward attaining that success?

- How does feedback or messages from others impact your learning?

- What are your strengths?

Self Awareness Resources for Students

Tortoise and the Hare Aesop's Fables

The Carrot Seed by Ruth Krauss

John Henry by Julius Lester

The Little Engine That Could by Watty Piper

Mirette on the High Wire by Arnold McCully

Wilma Unlimited by Kathleen Krull

Alexander and the Terrible, No Good, Very Bad Day by Judith Viorst

A Chair for My Mother by Vera Williams

How Many Days to America? by Eve Bunting

The Little Red Ant and the Great Big Crumb by Shirley Climo

Pancakes for Breakfast by Tomie De Paola

The Little Red Hen by Paul Galdone

Snowflake Bentley by Jacqueline Briggs Martin

D.W. Flips by Marc Brown

The Big Wave by Pearl S. Buck

The Book of Virtues by William Bennett

Call It Courage by Armstrong Sperry

The Diary of a Young Girl by Anne Frank

Island of the Blue Dolphins by Scott O'Dell

Julie of the Wolves by Jean Craighead George

Nothing Is Impossible by Dorothy Aldis

Sadako and the Thousand Paper Cranes by Eleanor Coerr

Sarah Plain and Tall by Patricia MacLachlan

Stone Fox by John Reynolds Gardiner

Reach Higher by Scottie Pippen

Wizards Hall by Jane Yolen

Holes by Louis Sachar

Hatchet by Gary Paulsen

Sky Pioneer: a Photobiography of Amelia Earhart by Corinne Szabo

America's Champion Swimmer: Gertrude Ederle by David Adler

I Can't Said the Ant by Pollly Cameron

Jackie Robinson by James Olsen

Veronica Ganz by Morilyn Sachs

More Than Anything Else by Marie Bradby

Start Something by Earl Woods

What Makes Me Me? by Robert Winston

Self Awareness Resources for Teachers

I Want to Be by Thylias Moss Bang,

The Power of One by Bryce Courtney

Habitude #5:
Courage

**Success is the
by-product of
taking risks,**

**not letting fear
hold us back, and
taking the plunge**

HABITUDE # 5: COURAGE

The importance of courage as a habitude became clear to me in a most unlikely way. Recently I took my young niece, Katherine, to a local water park famous for its monster-sized water slide. I watched her closely as she began to make the climb to the top of what seemed like Mt. Everest. Each footstep became slower, softer, and smaller as she crept closer to the edge.

As she peered over and looked down, she paused briefly; her fear apparent. Yet, with one deep breath, she looked at me, and took the plunge!

As I met her at the bottom of the ride (yep, I turned around and walked back down) her first words to me were, "Auntie A. - you missed it...that was the best ride of my whole life. You should have done it with me!"

Although these words did not give me the courage to take the plunge myself, they did get me thinking about the role fear has on living and learning. How many "rides" have I missed because I was too scared to take the plunge, step out of my comfort zone, or turned around too early? How many times have you let the "woulda, coulda, shoulda" stand in the way of taking the ride of your life?

Katherine's story teaches a valuable lesson about courage. Students are willing and able to take the ride and risk outside of school, but do not transfer that same willingness to plunge within the confines of classroom work. When confronted with risk and challenge, they hesitate as they consider the consequences of looking incompetent, struggling, or not understanding. Over their time, optimism turns to pessimism, embarrassment, and ultimately learning defeat.

My goal in this chapter is to bring the childlike mindset we see in amusement parks into the classroom where fearless learning is the norm rather than the exception.

Porch Pitch: Why Courage Matters

"All our dreams can come true, if we have the courage to pursue them." - Walt Disney

You can do nothing worthwhile without courage. Courage enables us to manifest something real out of a dream. Talent and skill need courage. It is the stiff backbone that helps lift the task of promoting, depending, and making good on our sense of purpose. There is no other way to reach your potential.

We want our students to use their imagination and curiosity to dream, but they must be willing and able to do the following in order for their dreams to become a reality:

- Envision and Dream

- Be willing to work

- Stay convicted and take a stand on what is most important

- Look for strength inside, not outside of themselves

- Get uncomfortable!

- Believe they can be bigger than they are

Our students don't need to make headlines or engage in sensationalized endeavors to become students of courage. They just need to be willing to do the work necessary to reach their potential. The following lessons and conversations explore what courage work is all about.

Million Dollar Conversation (Anchor Lesson):

When is the last time you used the word courage in your classroom? It's a magnificent word. It's a BIG word. Yet, it's a word that is difficult to define and teach.

For many, courage means people risking or giving one's life for others. These actions of heroism and bravery will always be deeply respected as they touch every one of us to the core. But what about everyday courage? Intellectual courage? What devoted actions made by ordinary people in ordinary situations would be considered to be courageous?

The answers to these questions are what I seek to quantify in this first lesson with students, helping them define for themselves the true meaning of courage.

Boys and Girls,

When I say the word courage, what do you start thinking about? What do you feel? What do you see in your mind? (I record their answers and images on a chart)

As students share probable stories of heroism and bravery, fictional or real, I acknowledge and validate how the world most perceives courage and courageous behavior.

At this point in the lesson, I share with the group several definitions of courage, each revealing a significant behavior or attitude such as taking risks, being confident, or facing a fear. Any quotes on courage can be used, but here are a few to begin the conversation with:

- Courage is not the absence of fear, but rather the judgment that something else is more important than fear. - Ambrose Redmond

- Success is not final, failure is not fatal: it is the courage to continue that counts. - Winston Churchill

- Courage is never to let your actions be influenced by your fears. - Arthur Koestler

- With courage you will dare to take risks, have the strength to be compassionate, and the wisdom to be humble. Courage is the foundation of integrity. - Keshavan Nair

- Personal mastery teaches us to choose. Choosing is a courageous act; picking the results in actions which you will make into your destiny." - Peter Senge

- Courage is not the lack of fear. It is the acting in spite of it. - Mark Twain

- Courage is fear holding on a minute longer. - George S. Patton

As you can see, boys and girls, courage is not one attribute, or a recipe, but it is a cluster of strengths. (The list of courage attributes comes from the student discussion of the quotes; the following is a representation of those discussions that I chart in this way.)

We display courage when we:

- Allow failure

- Learn from bad decisions

- Listen intently to ideas and opinions that differ from ours.

- Become honest with ourselves, taking responsibility for outcomes positive or not

- Remain confident in the face of opposition, internal or external

Boys and Girls, gaining courage is not something that happens in a day, a week, or even a year. It is an ongoing process throughout our lives. It is found not by looking for it, but rather from a consistent effort towards courage-building behaviors.

So, as we study these behaviors and attributes over the next few weeks, your job will be to recognize in yourself and others when you see courage work. We will be keeping a courage journal, so that both in and outside of school you have a place to record your observations

Let's start today. Take the next few minutes and create your first journal entry. Choose one courage attribute that you see in your own learning life. I will be keeping a journal as well and look forward to sharing my entry with you tomorrow.

I keep the journals handy at all times, so students get accustomed to linking specific behaviors and actions with the habitude of courage. As examples become more concrete, courage becomes a way of acting and being rather than an abstract concept of thinking. It is important you journal alongside your students, as you model the kind of reflection and conscious attention to behaviors you wish them to be aware of.

Lessons that Last: Continuing the Dialogue

Courage cannot be "mastered." It develops over time and with practice. The following courage lessons provide you with specific ideas and tools to build courage.

These lessons do not follow a prescribed scope and sequence. They can and should be, expanded and extended over days and weeks. These conversations keep the habitude alive and moving, so students link courage in their deskwork and their life work.

Lesson One: Looking Fear In The Face

"You gain strength, courage and confidence by every experience in which you really stop to look fear in the face. You are able to say to yourself, I have lived through this horror. I can take the next thing that comes along. You must do the thing you think you cannot do." - Eleanor Roosevelt

Fear. The word itself scares me. Say it …FEAR! Scary, isn't it? Yet fear is something we all have to face. It is the universal equalizer. Regardless of age, occupation, gender, or status -- fear has the power to make the strongest among us weak… if we let it.

This lesson is not about helping students avoid fear, but rather how to face it head on. Regardless of its nature, whether it is fear of failure, fear of rejection; fear of humiliation; or even fear of fear itself… facing your fear is the #1 quickest way to build courage.

I wonder what our student's learning life would be if these fears could be controlled and monitored? Let's listen in:

Good Morning Learners,

Something important to address in our conversations about courage, is the way successful learners handle fear. Let's talk about that today, shall we? My goal at the end of our conversation is this:

- *You will have new insight into how you look at fear and its role in your learning*

- *You will understand what is involved and expected in fearless learning*

- *You will have tools that you can use immediately when you see fear getting in the way of pursuing your goals*

Here's the deal. Fear is a reality for all learners. Getting A's does not make you a fearless learner - it is your attitude, mindset, and behaviors that will equip you to handle your fears. Courage is defined by how you handle fear.

Being fearless requires that we know ourselves, face ourselves, and more importantly, trust ourselves. When we are fearless, we're more likely to accept the existence of fear, we accept that things sometimes fall apart, and we move ahead anyway.

The more often we fail and recover, the more we learn how to be successful. It's when we fail and then fail to recover, that we get stuck in fear, and it becomes our master.

To be fearless learners, you must understand:

- *Fear is a natural emotion - even the most courageous among us fear something. The difference is they do not let the fear paralyze them.*

- *Get to know your fear(s). Accept it. Embrace it. By doing so, you can overcome it.*

- *Things will happen. It's inevitable. And you won't like some of those things, but you will deal with them when they happen.*

- *You are capable and smart individuals. Everything you need to cope is inside you.*

- *You will have friends and classmates who will support you. You cannot handle everything alone. A huge step in becoming fearless is knowing how to create a strong network of support.*

- *Messing up is not the end, it is only a step in a direction — you have the power to choose that direction — forward or backward… the choice is yours.*

When you face your fears, you begin to realize that things aren't as scary as you once thought. You become able to tackle bigger and better tasks and projects, even in the faces of uncertainty, intimidation, and even more fear!

In your courage journal today, I want you to write about one of your biggest fears. This will not be shared with the group unless you choose to do so.

Tomorrow's lessons will explore specific steps to help you accept and work through that fear, and explore the tools that give you confidence.

Lesson Two: Taking Action

"One courageous step at a time. We develop courage by doing courageous acts." – Aristotle

Wherever we see greatness, we are looking at the result of someone who had the courage to act. Without action there can be no change, and without change, there can be no improvement or growth. Fear can be immobilizing, but action sets change in motion. The best cure for fear is action. This lesson is about helping students through every step of action.

Good Morning Fearless Learners – We have had some great conversations about courage and fear. Knowing that even the most courageous still get afraid is helpful, but what I really want us to explore today is what tools we need to face that fear.

Ignoring it, denying it, avoiding it, only gives fear more power. I want to share with you one of the tools that I use to help me manage my fear, literally one step at a time.

One of my passions growing up, and still today is playing the piano. I loved to play, I did not even mind the bad notes, but I was terrified of the piano performance. Getting up on stage and performing in front of a large group absolutely terrified me. The fear of other people judging me and thinking about how I play, act, and perform was stopping me from moving forward with my skill. It was like a giant roadblock getting in the way of what I loved to do-play and perform.

The tool that helped me manage my fear during this time is what I call my FEAR GRADIENT.

Here's how it works:

I did not want to throw myself into my fear all at once, so I opted for smaller, less fearful tasks and used those to build a foundation of courage and confidence. I chose 3 or 4 levels of easier, less scary tasks. And like stepping stones, each level brings me closer and closer to conquering what I am most fearful about.

With piano, I knew my goal was playing at my school musical where my audience was BIG – all the school faculty, students, and my friends and family members. Level one for me was playing for a small group first. I would invite family and a few friends during practice so I would get used to an "audience." They would give me encouraging words and tell me that I could play for anyone! That gave me the confidence to move to Level Two- playing for a bigger audience at my church.

The piano was in the back, and I knew no one really was looking at me, so I could feel what it was like playing for a bigger crowd without as much pressure. Over time, I was able to confront the hardest fear — giving a high pressure performance for a BIG audience. Now, I am able to play for friends and family, church, and yes, even for BIG audiences. Fear did not stop me from pursuing my dream, in fact I love performing. Wanna hear a tune?

My point is this: I still get nervous, but I have been able to replace fear with courage; courage to know that I can actually do what I thought that I could never do. And you can do the same; baby steps are what it takes.

Student Assignment: Create a Fear Gradient. Have students identify something that they are fearful about doing. They can do this publicly or record their goal in their courage journal. Students can work with partners to help identify two or three "baby steps" that can be used as landmarks on their gradient to represent levels one and two. The assignment can take several weeks depending on how steep their learning curve is. The exercise can be shared accordingly over time. (See

Appendix for example)

Lesson Three: Get Uncomfortable!

"Be willing to be uncomfortable. Be comfortable being uncomfortable. It may get tough, but is a small price to pay for living a dream."- Peter McWilliams:

From an early age our students are taught the following:

Comfortable = good (pleasurable)

Uncomfortable = bad (stressful, unhappy)

In the 21st Century, safe and comfortable could be the greatest risk our learners face. Let's talk frankly about what being comfortable means in a 21st Century learning context - when students get too comfortable, learning just the basics, doing just enough to get by, they are at risk for:

- Boredom

- Disengagement

- Being unchallenged

- Complacency

- Getting Stuck

- Unwillingness to change

This courage lesson is a lesson in re-association, so when students experience discomfort, they recognize struggle as a natural and necessary part of learning. They know struggle sits at the doorstep of breakthrough. Courage is the weapon they need to fight complacency, conformity, and disengagement.

Good Morning Boys and Girls-

You know how sometimes I start the day by saying, let's get comfortable? Are you comfortable? Well today, I have a new question for you. When is the last time you have been uncomfortable? I don't mean the chair you are sitting in or the temperature of the room, I mean in your brain, in your learning. When is the last time that you felt stretched, challenged, discomfort?

I am going to ask you, no...require you to get uncomfortable, with learning that is.

Now, I know many of you are thinking that this does not make sense-why would Mrs. Maiers want learning for us to be uncomfortable? Doesn't she want us to succeed and be happy as learners?

I know exactly what I am asking you to do. I absolutely want you to feel successful and happy as learners. What I do not want to see happen is for you to choose easy tasks, to take the easy road, or to do the bare minimum to get by just so that you can feel comfortable.

Learning is hard; it even hurts sometimes because things don't go smoothly. This is where courage is needed. You have to become accustomed and comfortable in the times when things are not going smooth, when challenge is there, you have to learn to be comfortable when learning is uncomfortable.

Here's the important point: it is during the uncomfortable moments of frustration and despair that learners quit, saying I do not get it, I can't do this, and I don't care anymore. They do not have the strength or courage to stick it out and work through the work.

They are not comfortable with being uncomfortable — they just want to know the quick and easy solution.

Let's talk about that for a bit…

At this point I want students to share openly and honestly about an experience they have had during a difficult and challenging learning time, and how they responded and reacted in the mist of the struggle. Did they quit? Did they stick it out? What strategies helped, hindered? Students can choose to do this in their courage journal, or the reflection can be made public in whole group or small group discussions.

I wrap up this conversation in the following way:

When you see the word comfortable- I want you to associate these words with it...

- Boredom

- Complacency

- Overconfidence

- Stunted

- Closed-minded

As learners, you put yourself are at risk of falling into these learning traps when you do not expose yourself to challenge and discomfort.

When you start to feel discomfort, start telling yourself this:

- I am learning

- I am stretching myself

- My brain is getting smarter

- This is soooo good for me

- Growth cannot happen without discomfort

- My brain gets stronger every time I challenge it

If we do the same things every day, we are not really growing. We only learn and grow when we are challenged to expand our comfort zones, so I challenge you this week to BE UNCOMFORTABLE! Do something at least once a day that may make you uncomfortable and write about it in your courage journal. Let's brainstorm a quick list of learning possibilities to get you started:

- Talk to someone new today

- Ask a question in class

- Challenge something your teacher said (in a respectful way, of course)

- Try a new genre

- Teach a classmate how to do something

- Speak publicly - Ask for a few minutes to share or teach the class

- Learn a new skill or strategy

- Draw something

- Become a character-act out a scene in a book or movie

You build your courage muscle like any other in your body-the more you stretch it, the more you work it out, the stronger it becomes. Muscle and brain work require lifelong maintenance. Just because you lifted weights once-does not give you strength for life. Stretching and building your courage is a daily, lifelong workout! Happy lifting!

Lesson Four: Courageous Conversation

Any of this sound familiar?

Teacher reads the book. Teacher asks questions. Students (usually the same one or two) answer the questions. Lesson ends.

The dialogue here is safe; but the learning is at risk. Where is the courage? The courage to ask different questions, challenge the answers, defend alternate points of view?

Taking a stand for what one believes or thinks is one of most courageous actions our students can take, and they are "practiced" out of it. Students have become programmed to respond directly to us, bypassing the comments, ideas, and interpretations of one another. When students become accustomed to asking each other for reasons and opinions, to listen carefully to one another, to build on another's ideas, they demonstrate courage.

In order to get students to respond in deeper, more courageous ways, they need to begin listening to one another and offer their comments directly to each other rather than always through the teacher. This requires vigilant shifts in classroom discussion dynamics where the focus from teacher asks question-students answers moves towards learner ideas and issues.

To begin this shift toward courageous conversation, I use a strategy adapted from Frank Serafani's work, entitled YOU SAY, I SAY, SO WHAT.

This strategy has multiple goals: To get students to listen carefully, use what is offered as the foundation for their subsequent comments, and most importantly to take action on the knowledge gained as meaning is courageously negotiated in intelligent and respectful ways.

Good Morning Learners! Today we are going to practice what I call having a courageous conversation. We are used to having class discussions, and you are very good at paying attention and answering the questions I ask. The focus of today's conversation is different. A courageous conversation involves three very important attributes we are going to work on together:

The first is listening to one another. As each learner speaks, we are going to be working on actively listening to what they are saying, why they are saying what they think, and what we are learning from their ideas.

The second rule in a courageous conversation is pausing. Before we offer our own thoughts and comments in response to one another, I want us to pause long enough to reflect on what our classmates have added to the conversations so that we can specifically refer to what they have contributed. Only then will we be allowed to add our own thinking.

Finally, as we negotiate meaning through listening and responding to one another, we together make a decision on what we are going to do with this knowledge. We commit to an action together.

To help us work through these three step, let's think about structuring our conversation in this way:

- ***You say*** *- one of our classmates shares their thoughts and ideas about our discussion topic.*

- ***I say*** *- After pause and reflection we acknowledge what has been said while adding our own thought and opinion.*

- ***Now What*** *- Together we will decide what, if any action should or could be taken because of what we learned.*

This conversation tool can begin with a work of literature or be part of the daily curriculum. The important focus of the lesson is to get students to listen to one another and not just talk directly to the teacher all the time. The conversations may seem a bit inauthentic and mechanical; the flow will come with practice as students become more effective as a community of readers, writers, and communicators.

Lesson Five: Everyday Heroes

"I long to accomplish a great and nobler task, but it is my chief duty to accomplish humble tasks as though they were great and noble. The world is moved along, not only by mighty shoves of heroes, but also by the aggregate of the tiny pushes of each honest worker." - Helen Keller

We are a society of "hero worshippers." Adorations and devotion are given to those who survive 40 days on a desert island or display their life in front of a camera for millions to watch. It is no wonder students confuse idolism and heroism.

In this lesson, I want students to recognize what Helen Keller so eloquently spoke of – how heroism and courage come in our every day acts, not during sensationalized bouts of fame and fortune.

Good Morning Friends-

We have had some amazing discussions about the habitude of courage, haven't we? In this final lesson, I want to leave you thinking about courage in this way. Courage is not something "TO DO" like a checklist you create in the morning…Today, I will do my homework, make my bed, brush my teeth, and oh yes…do something courageous. Courage doesn't work that way. Courage is not a TO DO it is a TO BE. Let me explain. To get to where you want to be in learning or life is determined by your behaviors, actions, and attitude. Courage is represented in the kind of person that you will have to be to get through the tough times and to pursue your goals.

I have made a list of adjectives that represent my TO BE list in my courage journal. It is a reminder to myself of the kind of person I want TO BE everyday in every act, big or small. This list serves as a promise, almost a vow to become more like this person I want to be each day I wake up.

Mrs. Maiers' TO BE list:

- A better listener

- Open-minded

- Convicted

- Unafraid

- Curious

- Confident

- Flexible

I realize that every day my courage will be tested. As I learn and grow, I will use my TO BE list to guide my behaviors, actions, and attitude as I move forward through obstacles and challenges I face.

Who can guess what your final entry in your courage journal will be? You got it, I want you to create your TO BE list. Make it big, use powerful adjectives, and be specific! You choose the words that will influence the kind of courage you can have - be picky and proud!

Close

During the Great Depression, Thomas Edison delivered his last public message. In it he said, "My message to you is: Be Courageous! I have lived a long time. I have seen history repeat itself again and again. I have seen many depressions in business. America has always come out stronger and more prosperous. Be brave as your fathers before you. Have faith! Go forward!"

Edison knew then that courage is the force that propels us forward into and onto more powerful things. Courage, like all other habitudes, is not something you can "give" students. It is something that must come from within. As you strive to do what is right and best, it is my hope that these conversations show students that the decisions made every day are an investment in courage. There is no other way to reach their potential.

Courage Resources For Students

Somebody Loves You, Mr. Hatch by Eileen Spinelli

The Searcher and the Old Tree by David McPhail

Dex, The Heart of a Hero by Carolyn Buehner

Superhero by Marc Tauss

Princess Smarty Pants by Babette Cole

Jane and the Dragon by Martin Baynton

Flyaway Katie by Polly Dunbar

Augustus and His Smile by Catherine Rayner

Silly Billy by Anthony Browne

Sebastian's Roller Skates by Jean de Deu Prats

Brave Horace by Holly Keller

Walk On: A Guide for Babies of All Ages by Marla Frazee

Courage of the Blue Boy by Robert Neubecker

Is a Worry Worrying You? by Ferida Wolff and Harriet May Savitz

The Cello of Mr. O by Jane Cutler

Call It Courage by Armstrong Sperry

Color Me Dark by Patricia McKissack

Fear Place by Phyllis Reynolds Naylor

Guts by Gary Paulsen

Hatchet by Gary Paulsen

I Rode a Horse of Milk White Jade by Diana Lee Wilson

Oliver Button Is a Sissy by Tomie DePaola

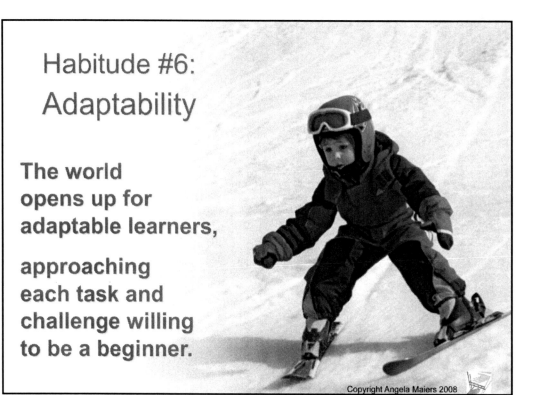

Habitude #6:
Adaptability

The world opens up for adaptable learners,

approaching each task and challenge willing to be a beginner.

Copyright Angela Maiers 2008

HABITUDE 6: ADAPTABILITY

Imagine a world that never changes. What would your life be like without the changes you have experienced over the last 20 years, 20 days…20 minutes?

We have a love-hate relationship with change. On one hand, we greet innovation and new development with open hearts and hands. But when it comes to being the one having to do the change, change becomes an enemy. Our students are no different. With steep learning curves thrust upon them, they cling to what is most comfortable.

Adaptability for the learner is more than just serving change - it is using change as a growth opportunity. In fact, with anticipation of change, you can control change. This kind of development requires robust adaptability. The world opens up for adaptable learners, as they approach each task, each challenge willing to be a beginner, approaching their learning and life with a beginner's mindset. These learners embrace challenge with openness, flexibility. Those who don't embrace change with adaptability usually get blind-sided by it.

Porch Pitch: Why Adaptability Matters

"It is not the strongest of the species that will survive, or the most intelligent. It is the one most adaptable to change."- Charles Darwin

As Darwin observed, this sentiment holds true in both biology and education. The concept of adaptability is not new as the pace and types of change we experience continue to grow rapidly. "In a global economy, workers need to be increasingly adaptable, versatile, and tolerant of uncertainty in order to operate effectively and efficiently in these changing and varied environments." (21st Century Learning)

Simply put, in our world, there is only one constant: change. And that's why the adaptable will survive and thrive in change.

21st Century learners must be able to:

- Respond favorably to change

- Handle complexity

- Critically and creatively solve problems

- Be willing to take risks

Persistent adaptability allows students to respond rather than react, reflect rather than remember, and evolve rather than atrophy.

Million Dollar Conversation (Anchor Lesson):

Boys and Girls,

Today's Habitude study is Adaptability. Take a minute and talk with one another about adaptability. Have you heard the word adapt before? Why do you think being able to adapt or be adaptable is important to successful learning/living? Students shared the following ideas about adaptability:

- *It is something animals do in their environments, like chameleons - they adapt to their surroundings, right?*

- *Adaptability is part of how animals survive and live.*

- *Dinosaurs are extinct because they couldn't adapt to the land or weather.*

- *People can adapt too, like during weather. They can go from hot climates to cold.*

- *When you adapt it means you change to better fit your environment or circumstance.*

You guys are right on! Adaptability is about change and how we view the changes we want or need to make. Those changes can be something from the outside, or something we want to personally improve from the inside. Being adaptable is a two-part habitude. First, you must be flexible and willing to adapt to the change. Having a positive attitude about the change is critical. Second, you must have the ability and the resources to handle or make the change.

Here's why working through this habitude together is so important. Adapting to any change is difficult, even if the change is a good one. Adapting means that in some way you have to do or be something different. The problem is, we like to be comfortable. We like to do things in the same way we have always done them. In our routines, we become comfortable and safe. Trying new things or doing something in a different way is hard work because you have to keep challenging yourself. If we continue to stay clear of change and hang onto what is easy and comfortable; we will never get better, or stronger, or grow. And besides, change is going to happen whether we're comfortable or not.

I want to share with you a story of my adaptability: (Share your own story here)

When I began running as part of my exercise program, for almost six months I ran the same route, at the same pace, sometimes even at the same time. I got so comfortable running the same route that it wasn't even hard for me anymore. The problem was, I was not getting stronger and better as a runner. The only way that I could get better was to adapt. So, here's what I did: I added challenge to my normal running routine. Some days, I would do hills, sometimes I would run faster, sometimes longer. Even though it was hard, the adaptations I used helped me become a better runner.

Champion learners are just like that. They never let themselves get too comfortable with what they know and do. They challenge themselves by continuously adapting. When they run into a problem, they love it because it means that new, smarter learning is ahead. They are confident that any problem they encounter can be handled. Adaptive learners are life-long learners because learning never stops. In every situation, there is always a way that they could do it better, smarter, faster. That is the kind of learner I know we all can be. Over the next few weeks, we are going to be learning and practicing becoming adaptive learners. The ability to adapt can be learned. As with most skills, it takes practice, practice, practice.

Here's what I would like you to do before we talk again. I want you to think of a time in your life when you have needed to make a change, like I did with my running. What helped you adapt? How was your attitude? What tools or behaviors helped you adapt successfully? Draw a picture to tell me a little about that experience. We will share those so we can learn from one another.

Lessons that Last: Continuing the Dialogue

Adaptability cannot be "mastered." It develops over time and with practice. The following adaptability lessons provide you with specific ideas and tools to build adaptability. These lessons do not do not follow a prescribed scope and sequence. They can and should be, expanded and extended over days and weeks. These conversations keep the habitude alive and moving, so students link adaptability in their deskwork and their life work.

Lesson One: Portrait Of An Adaptive Learner

A good friend of mine is a third-year medical school student. She came in excited about attending the best teaching hospital. I asked her how she was learning more there than during her previous experiences.

"The answer is simple," she said. "Before making rounds, the doctor will always go in and discuss what they can expect to see, what they want the students to notice about certain patients or situation, and then at the end of the day, there is a reflection and review on what was noticed. Now we go into the work knowing what to expect and what to look out for, so as we reflect on our work as learners, we can pinpoint the aspects of adaptability we are working towards practicing." We can do the same for our students.

Boys and Girls,

We know adaptability is important if we want to remain strong and powerful learners. In order for that to happen, in school and out, there are important things we need to be aware of. As I share a personal story about adaptability, I want you to pay close attention to the following: What challenges did I face? How did I handle those challenges? What behaviors and attitudes did you notice? After the story, we'll make a list and call it "Portrait of an Adaptive Learner."

Here's what happened:

My sister recently visited me. I knew she was coming, so I had prepared a special dinner for her and her family. I had carefully planned the meal for four extra people, made my grocery list, and had even begun preparing some of the food. Just hours before they arrived, some very good friends of mine dropped by. Even though I was excited to see them, I knew I had better make some changes to my dinner plans. Listen carefully to what I did, and see if you can pick out the tools I used to help me adapt.

I noticed I started to feel frustrated. I wanted to see my friends, but I was very stressed that my sister was already on her way. So, I said to myself, "This is no big deal. We will just have something different for dinner. I will save the food for tomorrow night."

Next, I thought of a plan to make something that would feed more people, but still be quick to fix. And I had all the ingredients I needed. By just a few additions to the menu from the pantry, and modifying how the meal was prepared (we went from a single meatloaf to lots of spaghetti), we had a whole new menu.

Let's look at what you noticed:

- I changed my thinking with a better attitude

- I problem solved without panic

- I recreated something from inventory on hand.

- I looked at things differently

- I recognized change was on its way, with or without my approval

I used some of my first dinner plans to help me with my new dinner.

After the story, students noticed the following attributes to make up their "Portrait of an Adaptive Learner."

Lesson Two: Problem-Solving Lessons from Goldilocks

Literature can provide a fun and easy context for explaining and exploring ways to handle problems in creative and adaptable ways.

Familiar tales are rich with problem-solving possibilities, and this lesson with Goldilocks is one of my favorites. Reading with or to children, the goal of this lesson is to brainstorm ways the Bears can be helped in managing their problem.

There are many models of creative problem solving and most rely upon four elements or stages. I use the following outline to help frame our discussion: 1) identifying problems 2) Report Out. Describe the Problem 3) Producing ideas; and 4) Implementing and evaluating solutions.

Stage One: Identify the Problem:

The bears' home has been broken into and there has been property damage.

Stage Two: Describe the Problem Reporter Style (5W's and H)

Who was involved? Papa, Mama and Baby Bear; Goldilocks.

What Occurred? Break in; Personal belongings and items disturbed; Stranger in the house; Porridge eaten or spilled; chairs sat in and broken; beds slept in; runaway girl.

Where: Home in or on the edge of woods.

When: Child entered cottage while the bears were in the woods.

Why: Goldilocks' curiosity, hunger and need for sleep.

How: Open Window. Goldilocks entered the house uninvited and escaped through an open window.

Stage Three: Produce Ways to Solve the Problem

What does the Bear Family Do Now? What Adaptations can they make?

These ideas were share by 2nd Grade (!) Students:

- Buy new locks for the door

- Get ADT (Alarm System)

- Buy a dog

- Surveillance camera (Sign of the times)

- The bears could contact the three pigs and find out how they deal with intruders! (This one gets my vote!)

Stage 4: Evaluate/Implement the Adaptations

Students can vote on the best adaptation and then plan the steps and resources needed to make the adaptation happen.

We culminate the discussion by comparing how this project could help them solve real life dilemmas, too. Once students learn the steps and tools that support adaptive thinking and problem solving, they can use these tools outside the classroom.

Lesson Three: Step Outside the Box

Regardless of level or grade, students have grown accustomed to having a set of rules or constraints – a box – within which to think. By the time a student is 15 years old, they will have completed over 1500 exams with right and wrong answers. What do you think that does to their problem solving capabilities? They have been taught to look for one right answer, when many may be possible.

Students develop a narrow-minded approach, with a push for one simple solution. We complain when rigidity sets in, and complain that kids do not "think outside-of-thebox." So what is the box? And what does thinking outside of it really mean? This lesson seeks to explore that with students.

One of the first lessons I teach my University students works great for introducing - both literally and figuratively - what ouside-of-the-box thinking is all about. This exercise is a classic, and the solution is said to have spawned the phrase. "Thinking Outside the Box". Ready?

In front of students, I draw nine dots (three across by three down)

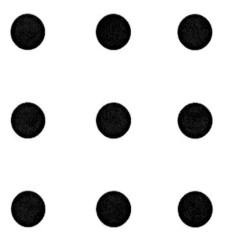

Then, I ask the students to join the nine dots together by using four lines only, and to do so without taking their pen of the paper.

So, how did you do?

I have found that the students enjoy this exercise and it is a great way to get the discussion brewing.

Here is just one of the possible solutions:

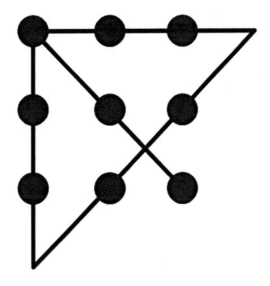

Lesson Four: Nurturing New Ideas Turning "Yeah, Buts" Into Yes, Hows

We have all been there. We come up with a new idea or a creative solution, and instead of our adaptability being celebrated, we hear these two little words... Yeah...but. Or in other words, "ARE YOU CRAZY?" that will never work. New ideas are fragile. The more creative, wild, or off-the-wall, the more fragile they become.

Fragile ideas need to be nourished. This lesson intends to keep those new and creative ideas moving forward.

It is far easier to kill an idea than to encourage it and turn it into a useful solution. I want students to be aware of how their language and response to new ideas can destroy discovery and breakthroughs.

I tell students that ideas are like gentle flowers. In order to bloom, the flower needs tender loving care. Even a slight wrong move could stifle the flower's ability to bloom. I make the connection that new ideas are like those flowers. In the beginning stages of growth, one wrong move and we kill it.

We must very careful with our new ideas; one wrong word has the potential to kill of the best thinking we are capable of. Even if the idea seems far-fetched, we will never kill the thought. Putting the words that could potentially damage or stifle a new idea on public display makes students aware of what to and what not to say. Here are some examples of our work.

To kill an idea, say...

- A good idea, but ...

- Too much work

- You could never do that

- They will never let us

- It is not my job

- Let's talk about it some more

- We've never tried it that way before

- We could never do that here

- We tried that already

To nurture an idea, say ...

- Wow, that could be very cool

- Yes, and ...

- That's a good idea/point/comment

- Great, let's try it

- How can we make time to see if it will work?

- What resources would we need to do it?

- Tell me more

- How can we make it work?

- Let's try it out

- What can I do to help this happen?

- I like it

- That sounds interesting, tell me more

Hopefully you will see there are many ways in which you can be constructive. There are even ways to encourage an idea without necessarily agreeing on action. Be on a constant watch out for putting down an idea too early without understanding the positive reasons for it being suggested.

Lesson Five: Learning How To Scamper: Lifelong Adaptability

Students assume that all problems are negative. The goal of this lesson is to view a problem as an opportunity and have them use their brain in a new or different way. Successful problem solving is adaptability in action. We have described the process of problem solving, but sometimes it takes a whole new approach, one students have not tried before. Sometimes, we have to stand back and try looking at the problem from different angles or perspectives. Enter: SCAMPER!

Developed by Bob Eberle, the changes SCAMPER stands for are:

Substitute - components, materials, people

Combine - mix, combine with other assemblies or services, integrate

Adapt - alter, change function, use part of another element

Modify - increase or reduce in scale, change shape, modify attributes (e.g. color)

Put to another use

Eliminate - remove elements, simplify, reduce to core functionality

Reverse - turn inside out or upside down.

The SCAMPER technique consists of a set of questions which, when answered, inspire newer ideas. It assumes that the answers we seek lie within the problem or task itself and by probing a little deeper we can find them.

SCAMPER serves as a framework of adaptability in actions. That helps you to think of changes you can make to an existing product to create a new one. You can use these changes either as direct suggestions or as starting points for lateral thinking.

Take Away:

Robert Sternburg, a leading authority on intelligence, interviewed hundreds of people and asked them what they considered to be the central characteristics of intelligence. As you can probably guess, they are the very things we have talked about with this habitude:

- Problem solving

- Ability to change

- Creative and critical thinking

- Being comfortable to risk

- Able to handle complexity

Sternberg wrote his own, "Intelligence is goal-directed adaptive behavior."

After these lessons with students, I want them to define intelligence with the ways the following students have adaptability:

- Being able to stretch your mind farther than you thought you could - Age 11

- Being adaptable makes you more intelligent because you can handle any problem that comes your way - Age 10

- How you can think of new ways of doing things - Age 7

- Important so you can talk what you know and apply it to something else you are learning - Age 9

- Shows you can think for yourself – Age 6

How do your students define this 21st Century Habitude? `

Close:

It is no accident that I included the habitude of adaptability last in the list. It is the central, and often most hidden factor to becoming independent and interdependent, relying on self and others. This habitude gives students not only an educational edge, but also an edge for living. This is what separates good from great, ordinary from extraordinary. By making sure this habitude is the foundation of future learning, we instill the wherewithal for our future adults to thrive and survive.

Adaptability Resources for Students and Teachers

Oh, The Place You Will Go by Dr. Suess

Thank You Mr. Falker by Patricia Pollacco

No easy answers by Donald Gallo

Who Moved my Cheese by Spencer Johnson

The Global Achievement Gap by Tony Wagner

The Legend of the Indian Paintbrush by Tomie de Paola

Snowflake Bentley by Martin Briggs

The Gardener by Sarah Stewart

A Story, A Story by Gail Haley

Joseph Had a Little Overcoat by Taback Simms

Sweet Clara and the Freedom Quilt by Deborah Hopkinson

Ox-Cart Man by Donald Hall

Weslandia by Paul Fleischman

Saving Sweetness by Diane Stanley

City Green by DyAnne DiSalvo

Make Lemonade by LaVaugnh Wolfe

The Richest Kids in Town by Peter Kehret

Rules of the Road by A. Bauer

Beyond the Western Sea by Avi

Babushaka's Doll by Patricia Polacco

The Girl Who Spun Gold by Virginia Hamilton

Five Brilliant Scientists by Lynda Jones

Fire on the Mountain by Jane Kurtz

The Girl Who Changed the World by Delia Ephron

Final (Starter) Thoughts

The Learners We Have, the Learners We Need

Thought you were done? Not quite yet, I have one more task before you leave our conversation. What we teach, our "checklists," has driven the discussions, debates, and decisions we make as educators for far too long.

We even define ourselves through the content we teach: Hello, my name is Angela and I teach literacy. I want you to leave today and everyday thinking about WHO you teach, and more importantly how you're teaching will influence WHO they are.

So, tell me about WHO you teach. Don't make this list quick just because you are almost done with the book. Really describe and define your learners. Tell me specifically what you know about those who sit before you every day. What are they like? What do you notice? How would you describe them? How do they engage both inside and outside your classroom?

Here's how others have answered these questions. I have categorized the responses by grade level — see if you notice a pattern emerging? WHO I teach?

High School/Middle School Learners were described as...

- Apathetic

- Disengaged

- Frustrated

- Unwilling to risk

- Disinterested

- Bored

- Inefficient

- Non-motivated

- Inflexible

- Shut Down

- "Faking It"

Elementary Learners (5 year olds...) were described as....

- Excited

- Energetic

- Inquisitive

- Eager

- Confident

- Avid

- Passionate

- Motivated

- Flexible

- Willing to risk

- Content with ambiguity

- Problem solving

- Strategic

- Curious

Notice any Habitudes?

Next question (ONLY QUESTION?):

Which learners do you wish your teaching produced?

In Jim Collins book, *Good to Great* he urged companies striving to become great to do the following: *"engage in dialogue, not coercion; conduct autopsies without blame; and build red-flag mechanisms that turn information into information that cannot be ignored."*

If your future hopes for your learners clash with your current realities, know two things:

- Learners come to us ready and equipped with the habitudes we most desire

- You now know how to get your learners there!

If you are reading this book, I know you absolutely have the skills and passion (and dare I say Habitudes) required by educators to prepare learners for their 21st Century challenges — so I leave you with this:

We can so do this!

And the answer to how is right in your hands and I know in your heart. I am amazed at how smart we can be together — please share your Habitude stories with one another. Use my lessons as a jumping of point. Reframe, refine, and most importantly share the conversations.

The knowledge we need for educational reform and change will not come in the form of scary statistics or scientific research (or even more mini lessons), it will come from these conversations. So, I ask, no implore you to be that change - live the habitudes that you wish your students to embody.

- Stay curious

- Use your imagination to seek solutions

- Persevere through the many challenges you face

- Stay self aware — notice what you model, monitor what you say, and seek continuous improvement in your practice

Embrace change by knowing you have the capacity to adapt, and go forth with courage believing in your power to influence.

Afterward

By David Armano

http://darmano.typepad.com

I have a confession. The story mentioned in the beginning of this book isn't just about my son Max, it's about me. Allow me to explain. I'm what most people would consider "successful." As a senior member of a digital marketing and design firm, my job not only provides for my family—it's both stimulating and rewarding. I really love what I do and feel blessed. But it wasn't always this way. From grade school to high school, and even my first year of college, I struggled to achieve the most modest of grades. Though I never "flunked" a class—I was far from what most teachers would regard as a model student. In fact to this day, I still have memories of teachers labeling me as "lazy", "unmotivated", "unfocused" and even "sloppy".

So when I took a look at Max's assignment—I immediately saw myself over 30 years ago. Max is a lot like me when I was a boy, he's highly creative—has a vivid imagination and doesn't find it easy to sit still. As I look at our future generation who will never know what life was like before digital—I can't help but wonder if there is an opportunity to evolve an education system which must now compete with the speed of digital media and social networking. I discovered digital in college and was an early adopter of computer graphics and the internet. Digital media including the internet dramatically influenced not only my career path—but also how I continued to learn. Initially it became a way for me to express my creativity— to design things without using my hands (I was never good at drawing a straight line—or like Max coloring inside them). The Web for me is profoundly educational. I learn by recognizing patterns, using my own intuitions to provide insights into why people do what they do. In business and marketing this is especially useful in identifying trends at an early stage before they reach the tipping point. In essence, I tap soft skills every day in my current life that were never nurtured, encouraged or even understood in school.

In fact, after reading Angela's "Habitudes" (Imagination, Curiosity, Persistence/ Perseverance, Self Awareness, Courage, and Adaptability) I am taken aback by how accurate these choices of words are—they almost perfectly describe the qualities that have best served me in life. It's important to make the distinction that these things can't always be taught. And we must acknowledge the educational system should not be held accountable for the paths people choose in life. However, educators must acknowledge that we now live in an age where we have spell check to correct our spelling and a surplus of information at our fingertips. These things will influence how we learn and the role education serves in our future. As a boy, I believed what the teachers thought about me, and I had to struggle to find my own way. I don't think it has to be this way.

Appendices

Habitude Awareness: The Unchecklist

Worksheets & Graphic Organizers

Resources on the Web

Success Quiz

Habitude Assessment

Your success in school and in life depends on the Habitudes you engage in. The following assessment asks students to reflect on and respond to your own Habitude development: Read each statement and have students think of a time or example when and where the Habitude actions were demonstrated. These questions can be adapted according to age and grade level appropriateness.

Imagination:

- Demonstrates an ability to connect the dots and see the "big picture."

- Utilizes foresight and intuitive perception as well as factual events to draw inferences.

- Recognizes supports and/or champions progressive ideas.

- Anticipates future trends or events.

- Envisions and/or predicts possibilities others may not.

- Dreams and/or talks about goals and the future.

- Identifies the multiple components of problems and their relationships.

- Utilizes logic and imaginative processes to analyze and solve problems.

- Imagines new or revolutionary concepts, methods, models, designs, processes, and/or technology.

Curiosity:

- Demonstrates curiosity and enthusiasm for learning.

- Using inquiry as a way of knowing.

- Ask questions beyond the text, assignment, discussion.

- Actively interested in new technologies, processes and methods.

- Welcomes or seeks assignments requiring new skills and knowledge.

- Encourages and promotes creativity and innovation.

- Modifies existing concepts, methods, models, designs, processes, technologies and systems.

- Develops and tests new theories to explain or resolve complex issues.

- Genuinely enjoys learning.

Self Awareness:

- Projects authenticity, confidence, conviction and passion.

- Demonstrate initiative, self-confidence, resiliency and a willingness to take responsibility for personal actions.

- Possesses unwavering confidence and belief in personal capabilities.

- Displays self-assurance.

- Asserts self in personal and learning life.

- Accepts personal responsibility for achieving personal and learning goals.

- Acts independently to achieve objectives without supervision.

- Expends the necessary time and effort to achieve goals.

- Establishes and works toward ambitious and challenging goals.

- Develops and implements strategies to meet objectives.

Perseverance:

- Takes initiative and does whatever it takes to achieve goals

- Bounces back after setbacks.

- Functions effectively and achieves results even in adverse circumstances.

- Admits mistakes and works to avoid repeating them.

- Accepts personal responsibility for achieving personal and professional goals.

- Functions effectively and achieves results even in adverse circumstances.

- Acts decisively despite obstacles, resistance or opposition.

- Anticipates, identifies and resolves problems or obstacles.

- Utilizes logic and systematic processes to analyze and solve problems.

Courage:

- Takes risks for the sake of principles, values or mission.

- Inspires others with compelling visions.

- Demonstrates an ability to make difficult decisions in a timely manner.

- Gathers relevant input and develops a rational for making decisions.

- Evaluates the impact or consequences of decisions before making them.

- Acts decisively despite obstacles, resistance or opposition.

- Accepts consequences of decisions.

- Willing to correct erroneous decisions when necessary.

- Stands by or defends rational for decisions when necessary.

Adaptability:

- Embraces and/or champions change.

- Responds promptly to shifts in direction, priorities and schedules.

- Demonstrates agility in accepting new ideas, approaches and/or methods.

- Effective in juggling multiple priorities and tasks.

- Modifies methods or strategies to fit changing circumstances.

- Adapts personal style to work with different people.

- Maintains productivity during transitions, and even in the midst of chaos.

- Expresses non-traditional perspectives and/or novel approaches.

- Synthesizes and/or simplifies data, ideas, models, processes or systems.

- Challenges established theories, methods and/or protocols.

Worksheets & Graphic Organizers

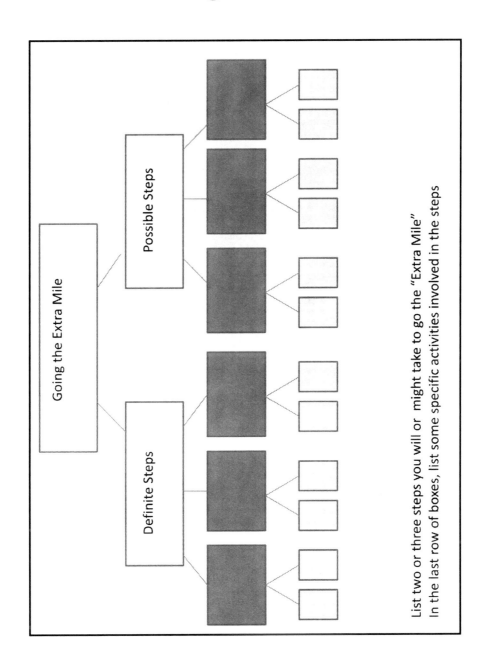

Personal Curiosity Inventory

1. Did you grow up being very curious about the world, the way things work, others?

2. What experiences have you had that fostered or inhibited your curiosity?

3. Who were your role models of curiosity?

4. Reflect on the last book you read or project you completed, what intrigued you most?

5. What questions do you have now?

Defining the Habitudes

Habitude	What is it?	Looks Like...	Sounds Like...	Feels Like...
1. Imagination				
2. Curiosity				
3. Courage				
4. Perseverance				
5. Self-Awareness				
6. Adaptability				

"How Come?"

Imagination Notes

What I See	What I Hear	What I Smell	What I Taste	What I Feel

Genius Questions

What if...?

I wonder why...?

If...?

What is it that...?

When is it...?

Who could...?

Is it possible to...?

When is...?

What could happen if...?

If it were possible...?

Are there...?

Why is...?

How...?

Where did...?

Do you...?

Is _____ the reason for...?

Can...?

Would you rather...?

What would it take to...?

Why is it that...?

How is _____ like _____?

If I _____, could _____?

Does it matter if...?

How can...?

What is your opinion about...?

Is it right to...?

I wonder when...?

I'm wondering if...?

How could it...?

Why are...?

Question Homework

☼ Find the most interesting question left unanswered by the reading.

☼ Identify the question the author was trying to answer.

☼ Write a question that will demand at least 10 minutes of thought to answer.

☼ Ask a question that is the "child" of a bigger question that can be identified.

☼ Identify the most/least important question and why.

☼ Write down three questions that bothered or stimulated you during the assignment?

☼ Write three hypothetical (compare, inferential,...) questions.

Assess and Conference

- Did you have a question before you started to read this text?

- How is asking questions working for you ?

- How do you plan to keep track of your questions?

- How does that question affect you understanding of the text?

- When you read_____. What question came to mind?

- What questions do you now have after rereading the text?

- Do you notice yourself asking questions when your reading does not make sense?

- How did questions help you to figure out meaning?

- Do you have questions that you expect the author to answer?

- If the author were here, what would you ask him/her?

- What will you do with the questions you still have left after reading?

- As I listen to your questions, I notice...

Question Typology

- Essential Questions
- Elaborating Questions
- Clarification Questions
- Hypothetical Questions
- Strategic Questions
- Probing Questions
- Planning Questions
- Unanswerable Questions
- Provocative Questions

Detective Notes: 5W's and an H

Who?

What?

Where?

When?

Why?

How?

S.C.A.M.P.E.R. Checklist

S: Substitute - *What could be used instead?*

C: Combine - *What could be added?*

A: Adapt - *How could things be adjusted ?*

M: Modify - *How could we add, change, or reform things?*

P: Put to Other Uses - *What else could it be used for?*

E: Eliminate - *What can be taken away or removed?*

R: Rearrange - *How can the pattern, sequence or layout be changed?*

Language of Adaptability

It could mean...

If we were to see it in another way...

This is how we could handle it...

This teaches us to...

We could...

An alternative might be...

Another option is...

If we took _____ and _____, we could...

I could use _____ and _____, and then...

Why don't we try this instead...

An alternative thought is...

From this perspective, I see that....

What if....

Fear Gradient

"Wow, I So Can Do _____
(Biggest Fear)
Level 3

"Now, I Can Do _____
(Biggest Fear)
Level 2

"I Can't Do _____
(Biggest Fear)
Level 1

Habitude Assessment

Teacher Reflection	Student Reflection
Imagination 1...............5 Because...	Imagination 1...............5 Because...
Curiosity 1...............5 Because...	Curiosity 1...............5 Because...
Self Awareness 1...............5 Because...	Self Awareness 1...............5 Because...
Perseverance 1...............5 Because...	Perseverance 1...............5 Because...
Courage 1...............5 Because...	Courage 1...............5 Because...
Adaptability 1...............5 Because...	Adaptability 1...............5 Because...

Awareness Inventory

- What did you learn? Is it what you set out to learn?

- Why did you want to learn this? What was your purpose for learning?

- Was your learning motivated by curiosity or necessity?

- How did the learning happen: By "doing" , "watching" , "studying"?

- Who else was involved in the learning process? How did they help or hinder?

- Where did the learning take place? Did you like that place?

- How did you know you were successful?

- Would you have like anything to go differently?

Strengths Assessment

- Who am I as a reader/learner?

- Can you describe your learning style?

- What do I see myself accomplishing in the next 5 year, 10 years, ...?

- What steps have you taken toward attaining that success?

- How does feedback or messages from others impact your learning?

- What are your strengths?

TRACK THNINKING:
Interactive Voice

- Make predictions
- Connect to personal experiences
- Visualize
- Identify the main idea
- Ask questions
- Recognize sequence
- Compare and contrast
- Identify cause and effect
- Summarize
- Draw conclusions
- Express opinions
- Identify and interpret the meaning of figurative language
- Identify and analyze problems and solutions
- Identify author's purpose

Self Awareness Worksheet

- My best trait is...

- I struggle most with...

- My favorite learning environment is...

- I help myself most by...

- What gets in the way of my learning is....

- I learn best by....

- I am interested in...

- My goals are...

Success Quiz

_____ Artist: All he wanted to do was to sketch cartoons. He applied with a Kansas City newspaper. The editor said, "It's easy to see from these sketches that you have no talent." No studio would give him a job. He ended up doing publicity work for a church in an old, dilapidated garage.

_____ Writer: Living in a car, trying to make ends meet, this writer submitted her first children's book to 27 publishers. She was rejected each time.

_____ Athlete: As a baseball player, he once held the record for striking out more than any player in the history of baseball: 1,330 times.

_____ Politician: defeated 7 times in run for political office.

_____ Athlete: missed his target 9,000 times, lost 300 games

Internet Resources

The Internet is constantly evolving and improving, adding new tools and cool sites for teachers and students to use in their learning.

I've created a page on my website where I continually try to add the best of these web pages:

http://www.angelamaiers.com/resources.html

Also, every Friday, I take the best sites I run across during each week and list them in a series I've dubbed ChalkTalk. You can find the archives of these posts on my site:

http://www.angelamaiers.com/chalk_talk/

Happy Surfing and Great Learning!

About Me - The Author
Angela Maiers

I believe that learning is a lifelong journey. I conduct workshops and training sessions helping learners of all ages develop their skills in critical thinking, reading, and communication. I challenge myself and others to always be striving to find and share big ideas in every million dollar conversation.

I work with teachers, principals, and school leaders on 21st Century learning competencies emphasizing technology, intellectual habits, critical thinking and problem solving strategies as ways to promote lifelong learning and success.

I am proud of my 20-year career in education, especially the years I spent as a classroom teacher. I now spend my time teaching, researching, writing, speaking, and conducting seminars across the country in the areas of literacy, learning, and 21st Century education.

My passion is to remove the obstacles to learning for all students; grown up students included. Whether it be online or offline tools, there is a way to make learning accessible for all. With the right conditions in place, lifelong learning is not a cliché, it becomes a reality. It is our responsibility as educators to do just that.

My website is a blog. Visit often at http://www.AngelaMaiers.com

You can also follow me on Twitter at http://twitter.com/AngelaMaiers

LaVergne, TN USA
13 March 2011

219818LV00002B/1/P